THOMAS MARENT | FRITZ JANTSCHKE

LIKE US

Encounters with primates

LIKE *Us*
Encounters
WITH PRIMATES

THOMAS MARENT

Text by Fritz Jantschke

FOREWORDS BY
JANE GOODALL
AND DIRK STEFFENS

WHITE STAR PUBLISHERS

Contents

Dirk Steffens: by monkeys, for monkeys, about monkeys

Monkeys are actually not particularly special. After all, there are millions of animal species and each one of these species is descended from the same single cells that at some time came to life in the "primordial soup." Stink bugs or hagfish have a history of evolution that is just as long and as fascinating as that of gorillas, chimpanzees and so on. Each species has developed with an equal footing on the tree of life. They are all in constant competition with each other.

Because in a biological sense life is without purpose, value judgments cannot be applied to it; there is no worthwhile life nor a worthless one. In terms of evolution all animals are equal. But that is not the case for us humans. A magnificent coffee-table book on stink bugs might be a worthwhile production but it would not arouse much interest. On the other hand if the book is about apes and monkeys we are interested, even very interested. This is because we are primates too. Admittedly we no longer have fur and we find our food in the refrigerator, but this does not alter the fact that Homo sapiens is basically a haplorhine or "dry-nosed" primate.

And this explains our interest: on seeing an ape, everyone intuitively understands that he or she is related to it. We feel a connection with these animals because there actually is one. And just as you feel closer to your parents, your children or your siblings than to strangers in the street, we care more about their fate than about that of other species.

We sense deep down in our genes that apes are not just any kind of animal. Not as far we are concerned. The tiny tarsier, the clever orangutan, the majestic gorilla, the social chimpanzee, the herbivorous gelada baboon or the skipping indri, the funny proboscis monkey or the noisy howler monkey, these are our relatives who live out there in the forest and jungle.

They bring home to us that we too are only a small part of nature.

Because their resemblance to us makes them so likeable, they are the best ambassadors that the threatened animal kingdom has. They bring home to us that we are only a small part of nature—and thus that monkeys are very special.

This book describes and explains both the great

> # We are the transition from
> # monkeys to humans.
>
> KONRAD LORENZ

HELP: The television presenter Dirk Steffens is pleased to be assisted by a chimpanzee as he presents a program.

diversity of these animals and their great beauty.

It is a book by monkeys, for monkeys, about monkeys and I hope that it will help to increase our appreciation of the wild branch of our family. Over 100 types of monkeys will be introduced in the pages that follow—quite a good representation. According to the current census there are over 450 monkey species on earth.

So in the future we look forward to seeing more photographs by Thomas Marent who approaches these wonderful creatures with noticeable respect as well as more texts by Fritz Jantschke reflecting the restless curiosity that has driven him to roam through forests, deserts and oceans for almost all his life.

Dirk Steffens

Following double pages:

8-9 *BABYSITTER: Black male Burmese snub-nosed monkeys looking after a group of children.*
10-11 *BEAUTIES: Golden-crowned sifakas in the constantly dwindling tropical forest of Madagascar.*

12-13 *A HOT BATH: Japanese macaque monkeys in a deliciously warm thermal spring.*
14-15 *THE THINKER: The pensive gaze of a bonobo to which we are more closely related than we may have thought.*

Jane Goodall: only if we understand...

Only if we understand can we care.
Only if we care will we help.
Only if we help shall they be saved.

I wrote these words on a poster that showed a chimpanzee in the Gombe Stream National Park where I started my research into wild great apes. Little Galahad looks at us with his large expressive eyes. The poster hangs above the desk of my old friend Fritz Jantschke, the author of this book. I gave it to him because I knew that he shared these beliefs with me.

When I started my research I had never been to university and I had no degree of any kind. After one year Dr. Louis Leakey, my tutor, offered me a doctoral position at Cambridge University. I was given to understand that my approach to chimpanzees was unscientific and unacceptable. Admittedly it was already generally accepted that chimpanzees were our closest relatives and it was considered scientifically legitimate to use them for medical experiments. I was not allowed to give names to the chimpanzees I worked with but only numbers. I was not to talk about their personality or intelligence; nor was I to indicate that they have emotions and

feelings in the same way as we do. It was pointed out to me that personality, intelligence and feelings were exclusively human attributes. Scientists wanted to have an impersonal relationship with their "research objects." Any empathy with them was taboo. My methods were strongly criticized. All the same I wrote my doctorate—and also mainstream articles on chimpanzee behavior for the "National Geographic."

Already by then I had realized how important it is to share information about animals and their behavior with scientific laypeople.

With time my unorthodox approach gained recognition.

People who were unable to experience the wonders of nature themselves should nevertheless learn to comprehend and appreciate them. So besides academic publications, I also wrote books and articles for a wider public.

With time my unorthodox approach gained recognition, even among scientists. When I first met Fritz Jantschke the rapport between us was

Do I prefer chimpanzees to people?
I prefer many chimpanzees to many people
and many people to many chimpanzees.

JANE GOODALL

JOY: David Greybeard was the first chimpanzee to make contact with the young research scientist Jane Goodall.

immediate. From the beginning of his career, after his dissertation on the behavior of orangutans, Fritz tried to publicize his knowledge not only among the restricted scientific community but also among the wider public. He has remained true to this approach and has done much to help people understanding animals. Because this is the only way—and we are in complete agreement about this—to persuade people to save endangered species and their habitats.

Together with Thomas Marent, a member of the International League of Conservation Photographers, he has now published this remarkable book. The Swiss photographer has managed to take pictures of more than 100 species of primates. As well as species that can be relatively easily caught in front

of the camera, there are also many that are rarely photographed in their natural habitat. This collection of quality photographs is brilliantly complemented by Fritz Jantschke's comprehensive information about the various primates. In this way this book can play an important role in protecting these animals.

More than ever we must mobilize as many people as possible and persuade them to become involved in nature preservation. The large tropical forests, home to most primates, are being sacrificed to the needs of a constantly growing human population. Millions of people are so poor that they cut down the last trees to keep their families alive. But worst of all is the greed and self-interest of those who have much more than they need and are only interested in making a profits; this is especially true of large international companies. Everywhere nature is under attack. We live in a time of massive extinction.

Many of the primates in this book are endangered, some of them very seriously threatened. This is especially true of the great apes in which we have a particular interest —if only because of our close relationship with them. The knowledge that we share over 98 percent of our genes with chimpanzees and bonobos will not in itself persuade anyone to help save them. But then you realize that they make and use tools, that they have a personality and a rich social life, the same emotions that we display, and a heart and feelings that can be appealed to. They share these properties with all primates (and countless other animals). Because of the damage we are causing nature, I no longer live in the forests that I love. Today research in the Gombe Stream National Park continues because we still have a lot to learn about our nearest relatives. But I also know that we shall not be able to save the chimpanzees if we do not at the same time improve the living conditions of people in this area.

Because of the damage we are causing nature, I no longer live in the forests that I love.

Thanks to our efforts the villagers now also help us protect the chimpanzees and their forests. They help us because they understand that the preservation of watercourses and the reforestation of the steep slopes will be beneficial to their own future. Meanwhile the "Jane Goodall Institute" and all its supporters have also become involved in other African countries to protect chimpanzees and their habitat.

I feel it is my duty to spread my message throughout the world. Since 1986, I am on the road about 300 days in the year in order to encourage as many people as possible to reflect about the consequences of our materialist lifestyle, about the consumer culture that started with us. I try to explain to them what it means when they buy products that have been manufactured under ethical conditions, without massive deforestation, without causing environmental pollution or poverty. I point out that we can save primates in faraway countries when we buy timber products that are certified by a trustworthy stamp of quality. Or that we should eat less (or even no) meat because of the enormous areas that are cleared in rain forests for cattle to graze or to grow grain to feed the constantly growing number of animals that are bred for human consumption.

But especially I try to reach young people. I want to make it clear to them that everything is not lost and that they can change things. The youth movement "Roots & Shoots" that we set up in Tanzania in 1991 is now active in over 130 countries around the world. We have members of all ages, from kindergarten to universities, where we have a strong presence. All groups have their own projects that aim to help people, animals and the environment. Only when the young people themselves take things into their own hands and understand that we must live in an environmentally friendly manner will there be hope for the future. After all, they are the next generation of parents, teachers, captains of industry, scientists and politicians. It is only when we have

Now we must redefine tool, redefine Man, or accept chimpanzees as humans.

LOUIS LEAKEY

won over a large number of such young people that we can hope to move in the right direction and live in harmony with nature.

Books such as these fascinate readers and encourage them to take part in the fight to preserve the wonder of nature. This is why I would like to thank Fritz Jantschke and Thomas Marent for having joined forces in this book project. I am convinced this book will help save our primate relatives and their habitat. But we must not stand still because the same is true of elephants , rhinoceroses and tigers that are being wiped out because of the greed for ivory or their bones, teeth and claws. It is our own future that is at stake.

I hope that you will join forces with us.

Jane Goodall

CONCERN: *Jane Goodall travels all over the world to save chimpanzees.*

Introduction

Fascinating, wonderful, lovable creatures

When in Africa you shine a powerful torch into the trees at night, you will sooner or later come across a pair of flashing eyes. Suddenly the reflecting flecks of light disappear only to reappear a few meters away in a completely different place. This game could go on forever: a small animal is making giant leaps in the trees.

But how should one arrange so many different species in a single book? After lengthy considerations and extensive discussions, it became obvious that the only approach was the zoological relationship, best from "the bottom upwards," from our more distant relatives to our closest ones. Linnaeus had already recognized this relationship and gave the name "primates" to the mammal classification that had man as "the summit of creation."

This term is (unfortunately) still valid today. But this classification is undergoing serious changes at the moment; in fact, something is changing every day. Today primates are grouped in two suborders, a sistinction that most of you will probably not be interested in: strepsirhini and haplorhini, the wet-nosed and dry-nosed monkeys. But we do not want to bother you any more with these little known, somewhat unappetizing terms that are hard to understand.

This classification is undergoing serious changes at the moment: in fact, something is changing every day.

You will find out everything you want to know about the correct classification of primates in the appendix of this book. All the species known today are listed there under their correct classification. There were 480 species when this book was written. Probably a couple more will have been discovered by the time this book is published.

To help the reader understand the classification better, we have divided it into four groups that the reader will know and be familiar with. We start with the so-called prosimians. These are in no way an immature species that has still to develop into "real" monkeys: they are highly-developed, admirable specialists. Just look at the next few pages, see them and read for yourself! Here we have grouped the tarsiers together, although this no longer reflects the most recent findings of zoologists.

> **The characteristics of a primate are its hands, its face and its brain. No other creature on earth has this unique combination.**
>
> SHIRLEY C. STRUM

LOVABLE: The large, expressive eyes and its wild shock of hair make this young Sumatran orangutan irresistible.

Tarsiers have their place in this chapter on the basis of both their appearance and their habit. The New World monkeys broke away from their relatives in the Old World very early on, which naturally entitles them to a chapter of their own. And in accordance with tradition we have divided the large group of Old World monkeys, in other words all the greater primates of Africa and Asia, into the Old World monkeys and the great apes. This results into four chapters that are distinct visually and in terms of content.

Each of these groups is accompanied by an introduction that will tell you fascinating information. In addition, there are fifteen other articles about interesting aspects of the life of primates. Here we encounter the varied, colorful, fascinating world of monkeys as promised by the second part of the title of this book.

The book covers species ranging from the tiny mouse lemur to the gigantic gorilla. All of them are related to us to a greater or lesser extent. We should not be embarrassed by this relationship. Monkeys are fascinating, wonderful, lovable creatures. To be interested in them is not enough.

We must also do everything in our power to ensure their survival.

Fritz Jantschke

Prosimians

BEAUTIFUL AND FAMILIAR:
The ring-tailed lemurs of southern
Madagascar are among the best known
and best researched prosimians.

Multi-faceted specialists and hedonists

When in Africa you shine a powerful torch into the trees at night, you will sooner or later come across a pair of flashing eyes. Suddenly the reflecting flecks of light disappear only to reappear a few meters away in a completely different place. This game could go on forever: a small animal is making giant leaps in the trees.

This little nocturnal animal is a so-called bushbaby. It is remarkable how it is able to finds its way in the dark without any difficulty. Galagos, as they are correctly known, detect insects in virtually complete darkness by using their giant, extremely light-sensitive eyes and large, very mobile ears. In order to catch their prey the monkeys make gigantic leaps with their long hind legs.

They are real hedonists. This is true of all the members of this group. That they are called "prosimian" is rather unfortunate and goes back to the scientific name Prosimia that Linnaeus gave these monkeys, which literally means "pre-monkey." The name seems to imply that they are immature creatures and maybe not even a "perfect" monkey. But this does not do these animals justice. They are as complete and viable as all the other primates.

Many primates have become brilliant insect hunters and hunt at night.

While many of them, including humans, could be described as "generalists," most of the animals in this chapter are high-grade specialists—from the galagos and loris of Africa and Asia to the lemurs of Madagascar and the tarsiers of Southeast Asia.

They have specialized most extremely where they share their habitat with other primates. It is their way of standing up to the competition. Many have become brilliant insect hunters, combined with the development of the sensory organs needed for hunting at night. These include large, highly light-gathering eyes and also a highly developed sense of hearing. Most of them have an outstanding sense of smell as well. This has largely been lost in the "higher" apes. Many prosimians mark their territory with special glandular

> # Of all the animals in the world it is man who is closest to the monkey.
>
> GEORG CHRISTOPH LICHTENBERG

A BEAUTIFUL STRANGER: The golden-crowned sifaka lives in a small remote area in the far north of Madagascar.

secretions or urine. In Madagascar many ring-tailed lemurs even have "stink fights" against each other. They swipe their bushy tail against the glands under the arms and wave it in the direction of their rival to release a strong odor. It is an effective way of putting their rival in his place without any physical contact!

There appears to be no set way of hunting insects. Many methods will lead the hunter to its prey. There are the jumpers who with their large eyes and ears hunt beetles that often buzz around in the air. The prey is caught with great skill and incredible mobility, then consumed.

Besides the galagos mentioned earlier, this group also includes the mouse lemur and tarsier.

The aye-ayes, a species of Madagascan lemur, are outstanding insect hunters.

In contrast the Asian loris, African pottos and Calabar pottos who belong to the same family have developed a diametrically opposed method. They move very slowly and climb

How lucky the monkey would consider himself, if only he could play lotto!

JOHANN WOLFGANG VON GOETHE

SUCCESSFUL: This fat-tailed dwarf lemur has obviously discovered some delicious fruit on its nocturnal foray.

steadily through the branches, catching sleeping spiders, reptiles and frogs. The aye-ayes that belong the group of Madagascar lemurs are outstanding insect hunters. Almost 39 in (100 cm) long, including the tail, they have specialized in extracting grub worms from wood. With their extremely long, withered-looking middle finger they tap the dry branches and use their enormous ears to hear if there are cavities beneath the bark. Then with their powerful teeth they gnaw at that spot before pulling the delicious prey out with the hook on the middle finger. As unusual as their food

gathering is the fact that aye-ayes build sleeping nests of about 2 ft (60 cm) in diameter. This is also where they give birth and bring up their young. If there was a competition for the most unusual representative of the primates, the aye-aye would win by a long way.

Most prosimians are loners or at best live in pairs or small groups. But in the case of the Madagascar lemurs there are a few kinds that live in really large groups. In fact, the ring-tailed lemurs frequently found in zoos have developed a special social system that is decidedly matriarchal. These differences are not limited to

their social behavior. The prosimians also differ enormously in body size and weight. While the galagos and loris are relatively small and light, ranging from 2 oz (50 g) for the dwarf galago to 41/2 lb (2 kg) for the greater galago and potto, in the case of the lemurs, besides the tiny mouse lemur, there are some very large types.

In terms of diversity, the Madagascar lemurs are the leaders among the primates.

The indri reaches a height of 311/2 in (80 cm) and weighs as much as 16 lb (7 kg). Before humans made their appearance on the scene there were even lemurs the size of a gorilla.

In terms of diversity, the Madagascar lemurs are undoubtedly the absolute leaders among the primates. They have developed a greater variety of survival strategies than all the other primates put together. For instance, there are the mouse lemurs that hunt insects by climbing quickly and leaping while the dwarf lemurs are slow climbers. Yet other types resemble Old World monkeys or Catarrhini in size, lifestyle and varied diet. Apparently in the course of their evolution lemurs were not under such high competitive pressure as other prosimians. The tarsiers of the islands of Southeast Asia occupy a special position. Like the galagos and mouse lemurs, these primates hunt insects at night and they are a kind of transition between the loris and lemurs on the one hand and the higher apes on the other. Based on the latest classification, they are grouped with the latter in

JUICY: Fork-crowned lemurs love tree sap. They gnaw the bark to get to this much sought-after delicacy.

the suborder "dry-nosed primates" or haplorrhines. They are highly specialized primates that according to recent findings perhaps only became nocturnal insect hunters secondarily. They are all fascinating specialists.

BROWN AND BLACK
Eulemur macaco

▪ North Madagascar

A female black lemur and, below, the male. In no other primate species are the two genders so different in color as in this one. They live in mixed groups of up to fifteen individuals (top and bottom left).

PHOTOGENIC
Eulemur macaco

▪ North Madagascar

Reserved but not afraid, this female black lemur looks at her distant relative the photographer, adopting the perfect pose for a photograph (right).

Like man, they manifestly feel pleasure and pain, happiness, and misery.

CHARLES DARWIN

A female ring-tailed lemur, self-confident as is typical of this species. Ring-tailed lemur groups are led by a female (right).

ALERT
Eulemur coronatus

▪ North Madagascar

Curiosity is a typical characteristic of all primates, not only of this female crowned lemur. Her red-haired partner behaves no differently (bottom left).

ABOUT TO GO
Eulemur coronatus

▪ North Madagascar

This crowned lemur is about six weeks old and therefore old enough to venture forth on its first foray in the neighborhood, away from its mother's breast or back (bottom right).

INDEPENDENT
Lemur catta

▪ South Madagascar

The ring-tailed lemur baby is weaned at the age of three months and by the time it is six month old it will be independent. But it will only be fully grown when it is eighteen months or two years old. Its lifespan in nature is about twenty years but in zoos some individuals have even lived beyond the age of thirty (left).

WELL LOOKED-AFTER
Lemur catta

▪ South Madagascar

The ring-tailed lemur baby is looked after by other females in the group as well as by its mother. When it is born—after a gestation time of four and a half months— the ring-tailed lemur has blue eyes that gradually change to orange (top right).

PROPRIETORIAL
Lemur catta

▪ South Madagascar

Ring-tailed lemurs mark their territory with a secretion produced by an underarm gland. That is what this one is about to do with its proudly raised tail (bottom right).

Propagation

How did the lemurs arrive in Madagascar?

Animals that have no competition can easily adapt to various habitats and develop in a different form. That is exactly what happened to the lemurs in Madagascar. But how did they end up on this tropical island that is over 300 miles (500 km) away from Africa? When the island of Madagascar separated from the continent 150 million years ago, there were no primates. The "leap" onto the island must therefore have taken place later. But even the best swimmers—and primates are not—could not travel such a distance. It is possible that the first ancestors of the lemurs used a kind of raft, as did other mammals of Madagascar which arrived on the island a long time after it first came into being.

And how did the New World monkeys arrive in South America? When the first primates arrived on the continent, it was still an island because the Central American land bridge did not yet exist. So for a long time it was thought that the monkeys had arrived directly from Africa over 50 million years ago. At that time the continents were not some 930 miles (1,500 km) apart from each other as they are now but only 300 miles (500 km) apart, and the ocean currents at that time were westward. So small primates on tree islands could have been driven there by the currents.

But according to more recent findings, monkeys probably arrived from the north. During a global warm period primates arrived in North America across the Behring Strait from Asia and in Scotland and Greenland

STILL COMMON: The beautiful ring-tailed lemurs with their striking tails are widespread throughout the south of Madagascar and live in a number of protected regions. Nonetheless their numbers have decreased in recent years.

from Europe. Sea levels were very low at the time, so small animals could easily have made their way across islands to arrive in South America. The separation must have happened very early on because the New World monkey is very different from the Old World monkey.

It is easy to explain why Japanese macaques live so far away from other monkeys. In the past primates were much more widespread. When conditions turned colder they were able to remain there because Japan's island climate was milder than the mainland. But it is quite a different situation with the Barbary apes of Gibraltar and the hamadryas baboon on the Arabian peninsula. In both these cases it is thought that humans must have moved their relatives to a new habitat.

RARE: The golden-crowned sifaka in northwest Madagascar has been classified as under serious threat because of the destruction of its habitat and because it is even hunted in some places.

VERY VARIABLE
Varecia variegata

▪ East Madagascar

The striking pattern of the black and white ruffed lemur can vary enormously. All subspecies are more or less under threat because their habitat has shrunk considerably (left).

COMPLETELY RELAXED
Varecia rubra

▪ Northeast Madagascar

A typical red muffed lemur. Although these beautiful creatures are hunted and their habitat is shrinking dramatically, they love resting and do so a lot—for about half the day, according to one study (right).

IMPRESSIVE
Indri indri

▪ Northeast Madagascar

With a sitting height of 30 in (75 cm) the indris are the largest prosimians. The tail is still only a short stump although—or perhaps because of it—they move incredibly elegantly in the jungle canopy (left).

A GLARING LOOK
Indri indri

▪ Northeast Madagascar

Light eyes are unusual and they make the indri's glare even more penetrating. In primates that are visual creatures it is also a form of communication: here a little threatening (top right).

QUAINT CALLS
Indri indri

▪ Northeast Madagascar

The morning territorial calls are eerily beautiful and are among the most unforgettable sounds to be heard in the Madagascar rain forest. Unfortunately this is increasingly being cleared (bottom right).

Night is not only for sleeping

Among the primates the differences are clearly defined. A primate is either active during the day (diurnal) or during the night (nocturnal). There are no border-crossers who can be out and about at all hours in the way that many hoofed animals and predators can. The Old World monkeys including the great apes are exclusively diurnal. At night they sleep and that is all. Among the New World monkeys there is one exception, the night or owl monkey. To be exact, there are actually eleven exceptions, because the *Aotus* genus, which until recently only included one species, has lately been found to contain eleven species, based on genetic differences. Tarsiers and all the prosimians of the loris and galago species are only active at night.

The situation among the Madagascar lemurs is less clear. Most smaller species, from the mouse lemur to the dwarf lemur, from the sportive lemur to the aye-ayes, are nocturnal creatures. The larger "real" lemurs who live in groups, from the ring-tailed lemurs to the sifakas and indris, are diurnal. In the morning they go out and lie in the sun for hours in order to soak up the warmth. Also it is not uncommon to see nocturnal sportive lemurs and fork-crowned lemurs sitting at the entrance of their sleeping cave when the sun rises. Without this external heat supply many lemurs would experience problems with their energy balance.

Most monkeys just look for any old place to

SHADY CHARACTERS: Of all the higher apes, only the night monkeys of South America have adapted to a nocturnal lifestyle.

sleep—if possible where they will be safe from enemies—undisturbed for twelve hours. Baboons prefer trees to sleep in, hamadryas baboons and gelada baboons sleep in niches on rock faces. Only chimpanzees, gorillas and orangutans build their own sleeping nest every night. They choose a suitable spot in a tree top—gorillas prefer to sleep on the ground. Using their hands, they bend twigs and hold them in place with their feet to form a sufficiently large platform on which they can sleep comfortably. Aye-ayes build tree nests like squirrels. They not only sleep there at night but they also give birth there. When the parents go and search for food, the young aye-ayes stay in the nest. This is very unusual because usually primates take their babies with them everywhere.

A LIE-IN: Sportive lemurs sitting at the entrance of their den in order to soak up some sun. After all, for them it is now bedtime.

A BIG LEAP
Propithecus verreauxii

▪ Southwest Madagascar

When the white sifaka is forced to move on the ground instead of in the trees (which is very rare), it does so by leaping very elegantly on two legs. These beautiful athletes are very widespread and only a near-threatened species, in spite of the clearing of the dry forests in which they prefer to live (left).

STRIKING
Propithecus coronatus

▪ Northwest Madagascar

With their unusual black and white pattern and their pale eyes the crowned sifakas are among the most striking primates. Like all sifakas they feed mainly on leaves. There is no shortage of leaves in the forests where they live but this habitat is constantly being eroded so that they are considered a threatened species (right).

PENETRATING GAZE
Propithecus verreauxii

▪ Southwest Madagascar

No one can resist the gaze of these pale green eyes. The eyes of the baby, which moves from its mother's breast to her back at the age of three months, are already almost as large as its mother's. The white sifikas are predominantly diurnal.

Not only people have a personality and are capable of thinking and experiencing emotions such as joy and sadness.

JANE GOODALL

THOUGHTFUL
Propithecus diadema

▪ Northeast Madagascar

Like all folivores, the diademed sifikas have a particularly long intestine and must give it a lot of time to digest the cellulose-rich food. This is why they always take a break even during the day (left).

STRIKING
Propithecus tattersalli

▪ North Madagascar

The golden-crowned sifika was only discovered in 1974 and fourteen years later the new species was named after the man who discovered it. They live both in monogamous pairs and mixed groups. In groups usually only one female reproduces (bottom left).

COLORLESS
Propithecus candidus

▪ Northeast Madagascar

It is not only the fur of the silky sifika that is the least pigmented of all the primates. Their skin also continues to lose further pigmentation with increasing age as can clearly be seen in the fingers and toes of the mother (bottom right).

One of my greatest challenges was to photograph the silky sifikas in the Marojejy National Park. These animals are among the rarest primates in the world. Admittedly the groups are quite tame, that is they are used to people, but the terrain is so steep and rugged that it is almost impossible to follow the animals. On this occasion I learned something that I found quite interesting: the females are said to be receptive only one day every two years.

THOMAS MARENT

Naming

What is your name ...

In Madagascar zoologists constantly have to find new names for newly discovered mouse lemurs. Until the end of the 20th century there were only four known species of the smallest primate. Since then on average a new species has been discovered every year. So far: nineteen in all. Besides such familiar names as *murinus* (mouse-like), *rufus* (reddish) and *griseorufus* (grey-reddish) there are a few others, named after distinguished researchers in Madagascar, such as the *berthae*, named after the Madagascan primatologist Berthe Rakotosamimanana, and the *jollyae*, named after the famous ring-tailed lemur specialist Alison Jolly. The most original tribute was in 2005 to Steve Goodman, who had worked for many years in Madagascar for the Natural Science Museum of Chicago. Goodman's mouse lemur, which at only 2 ounces (50 grams) is one of the smallest, is not called *goodmani* but *lehilahytsara*, from the Madagascan word for "good man."

Most names that are Latin or Greek have been inspired by physical characteristics, such as *Microcebus* = dwarf monkey for the mouse lemur, *Rhinopithecus* = proboscis or long-nosed monkey (the "right" long-nosed monkey is called *Nasalis* in Latin, that is, "with a nose") or *Ateles* = "thumbless" for the spider monkeys. Local names have rarely been adopted by science. Thus instead of adopting the Bantu name for chimpanzee which meant "pretend man," scientists called it *Pan troglodytes*, "god of shepherds liv-

DOUBLE NAME: *The scientific name of the aye-aye monkey,* Daubentonia madagascariensis, *honors the French naturalist Louis-Jean-Marie Daubenton and the island on which it was discovered, Madagascar.*

ing in a cave." The name langur is derived from the Sanskrit *langulin* which meant "having a long tail." Orangutan means "forest man" in Indonesian. The scientific name for these creatures is completely different. The South American Uakaris are an unusual exception. Both their popular name and their generic name *Cacajao* is derived from (different!) Indian languages.

An officially recognized scientific name does not get changed and it always refers to a particular species. But in the case of popular names the situation is rather confused. Often it would be better to change them. East lowland gorillas are in reality a sub-species of the mountain gorillas. So it would be more correct to call them West mountain gorillas.

ORIGINAL SPECIES NAME: Lehilahytsara *is the species name of this handsome mouse lemur. In the Madagascan language it means "good man," honoring the American scientist Steve Goodman.*

We have so much to learn about this astonishing animal that who knows what secrets we shall unravel in the future about the aye-aye's magic finger.

GERALD DURRELL

CHEEKY
Galagoides zanzibaricus

▪ East Tanzania, Zanzibar

The Zanzibar dwarf galago is one of the smallest primates, 16 inches (40 cm) long at most, half of which is the tail. It finds most its insect food on the ground (top left).

BIG EYES
Galago senegalensis

▪ Africa (Senegal to Somalia/Kenya)

The Senegal galago goes hunting at night, making giant leaps to catch the insects. Its large ears help the bushbaby to locate flying beetles while leaping about (bottom left).

CHUBBY
Nycticebus coucang

▪ South Thailand, Malaysia, Sumatra

At night the Sunda-Pumplori climbs slowly and cautiously along tree branches in search of fruit. Unlike the galagos and tarsiers, it is not really interested in consuming insects or animals (top right).

BIG EYES
Carlito syrichta

▪ Philippines

Besides its large eyes, typical of all the representatives of these highly specialized primates, the Philippine tarsier is notable for its long fingers. The scientific name Tarsiidae *is a reference to this feature,* Tarsius *meaning tarsus or ankle bones (bottom right).*

Food

It need not always be caviar

Primates are predominantly vegetarians. Usually they prefer what the plants and trees have to offer: ripe fruit and seeds. Chimpanzees as well as baboons, rhesus monkeys, spider monkeys and ring-tailed lemurs know which particular tree in their territory has delicious fruit and gather there. The fruit does not have to be sweet. For instance, wild figs that are very popular with rodents and birds are certainly not to our human taste. And acorns, the main nourishment of the Barbary apes that live in the Atlas Mmountains would certainly not be to our taste either.

Flowers, buds, young leaves, roots and tubers are also on the menu of vegetarian monkeys. But there are also several specialists among them. Africa's Angolan colobus (guerezas) feed almost exclusively on leaves as do Asia's colobines (langurs, doucs and proboscis monkeys). They have a chambered stomach in which this hard-to-digest food is processed with the aid of bacteria. The sifika lemurs and the howler monkeys have adapted similarly. The bamboo lemurs of Madagascar have specialized even more because like the Asian pandas they feed predominantly on bamboo. While these have found an ecological niche, the Ethiopian gelada baboons that live in the mountains only have grass to feed on.

Meanwhile the callitrichids of South America

EXTREME FOOD SPECIALIST: The grey bamboo lemur feeds almost exclusively on bamboo, which is extremely difficult to digest.

have gone their own way. They gnaw away at the bark of trees and then lick up the tree sap that oozes out. They also like to hunt insects, small reptiles and amphibians. Most nocturnal primates, owl monkeys as well as tarsiers, loris and galagos, and in Madagascar the mouse lemur as well as all the other small lemurs, are insect hunters. The bizarre aye-aye hooks beetle larvae out of trees using its spindle-shaped finger and long claws.

Almost all "generalists" among monkeys take their protein in the form of insects, bird's eggs and reptiles. Chimpanzees and baboons go even further: they have been known to devour a gazelle or bushbuck fawn. Chimpanzees, on the other hand, like to hunt colobus monkeys.

EXPERTS: Found only in Southeast Asia, tarsiers are even more specialized than the galagos in nocturnal insect-hunting

New World monkeys

CURIOUS OR DISTRUSTFUL:
Like the gaze of this monk saki,
much of the life of New World
monkey is still unknown.

New World monkeys

Resourceful forest-dwellers with quirks

Monkeys in the Amazon rain forest are hard to observe. At every step there is the risk of being caught by a branch or sinking down to the knees in the water. The tree canopy is so dense that animals can hardly be distinguished. This is especially true of monkeys, which move from tree top to tree top at great speed.

Fortunately we are sometimes guided by the sound of howling: howler monkeys. First the males start singing, then all the members of the troop join in. Howler monkeys are so engrossed in their concert that slowly-moving humans can observe them in peace. Then we notice a characteristic that only a few primates in South America have developed: a prehensile tail. Callitrichids are equally elusive in the rainforest. But in contrast to the howler monkeys, which always move in large troops, they swing about in the tree tops like squirrels. These are just two of the many lifestyles of the new world monkeys.

About 55 million years ago the New World monkeys broke away from the other primates and went their own evolutionary way. They are so distinct in body type and behavior that they are treated as a group in their own right. At first sight they are distinctive for a particular feature that has inspired their scientific name Platyrrhini, meaning "broad nosed." In fact the nasal septum is so thick that the nostrils do not point forwards but to the side. To see such a nose close at hand you will have visit a zoo.

No New World monkeys have ever left the original habitat of primates.

In the wild, in Central and South America, it is clear that the animals moving about high up in the tree canopy can only be New World monkeys.

Unlike a few of their relatives in Asia and Africa, no New World monkeys have ever left the original habitat of primates. All live in the forest as they always have. They live predominantly in the vast rain forest of the Amazon region where the different tree formations range from mountain forest to dry "cerrado" forest and riparian forest. The only exceptions are the capuchin monkeys which live on the coast where they hunt crabs.

There are thirteen species of monkeys (around the Yacari river in north-eastern Peru), and for me the red uakari is the most beautiful.

MARK BOWLER

RELATIVELY: The red uakaris certainly do not see themselves as ugly. Nevertheless these bald, red-faced creatures are very unusual.

It is not only the relationship to the ground but also the feeding habits of these individuals that is unusual. Like most primates, the menu of these South American individuals is predominantly vegetarian. Fruit, seeds, buds and flowers make up their staple diet. As a result the sakis and the uakaris have developed a particularly powerful bite that enables them to crack hard-shelled fruit. The various varieties of howler monkeys and woolly spider monkeys have concentrated more on leaf eating, albeit not quite as much as the leaf monkey of the Old World. Many callitrichids and owl monkeys have taken a different path, supplementing their diet with insects.

Colorfulness is the exception among New World monkeys.

Callitrichids improve their diet with an important nutrient: tree sap. With their sharp incisors they gnaw through the bark at a good place and lick up the resin oozing from the tree. They are the smallest of the "greater" primates.

It is remarkable that we only perceive as charming those monkeys that show the least resemblance to people. ALFRED BREHM

LARGE-EYED: The black-headed species of owl monkey from Peru. The large eyes indicate that owl monkeys are nocturnal.

Many weigh barely more than 3 1/2 ounces (100 grams). None of the nearly fifty varieties weighs as much as 2 1/4 pounds (1 kilogram) and most of them are less than 1 pound (0.45 kilograms). Even the titi monkeys and squirrel monkeys are not much bigger. Only the woolly monkeys and howler monkeys, the spider monkeys and woolly spider monkeys reach the size of Old World monkeys, and their maximum weight is much less, just 33 pounds (15 kilograms).

To adapt to life in the trees, some New World monkeys have developed their prehensile tail as a fifth hand, sensitive enough to grab even a small nut and strong enough to hang from safely. The capuchin monkey's tail is not as developed because it can only use it as a support. But spider monkeys and their relatives such as woolly monkeys and howler monkeys can hang from just the tail.

Apart from the uakaris with their bald heads and bright red faces, colorfulness is the exception among New World monkeys. This is why some of them have striking hair: there are many varieties with either a conspicuous beard, a thick head of hair or a bushy, densely hairy tail that is their distinctive physical feature.

LUXURY: The brown or woolly
monkey from Colombia has
unusually dense fur that it does
not really need.

The "invention" of fingernails instead of claws
has changed the behavior of callitrichids. For these
lightweight individuals it is often better to climb,
like squirrels do. Another unusual feature of these
dwarf monkeys is that they usually give birth to
twins (single births are the rule among all the
other greater apes) and it is not the mothers but
the fathers who carry the babies.

The number of New World species has risen to over 150, almost four times as many as before.

Because of these unusual features, callitrichids
used to be compared with the "capuchin type"
monkeys. Today they are divided into four families.
One of the earliest is the owl monkey, the only
nocturnal "greater" apes. Although they are almost
indistinguishable in appearance, they have been
divided into about a dozen species, based on origin
and genetic criteria. And quite rightly too—if owl
monkeys from various parts of the world were kept
together, they would not reproduce.

Because of the numerous "new" owl monkeys,
titi monkeys and callitrichids, the number of
species has risen to over 150. That is almost four
times as many as before. This large number is
linked to an amazing detail: most of the New
World monkeys are afraid of water and cannot
swim. The fact that the Amazon rain forest is
crossed by so many rivers has resulted in the
development of many individual species: each
little island has its inhabitants with their own
characteristics. Whenever such a microcosm is

SLENDER: Geoffroy's spider monkey is very slim, like all
its relatives.

destroyed, one of the species will become extinct.
That is especially true for all the monkeys of
the Atlantic rain forest in Brazil. This has been
reduced to less than ten percent of its original area
so the lion tamarin and other species in this region
are seriously endangered.

THOUGHTFUL
Lagothrix cana

▪ Amazon region of Brazil,
Southeast Peru

*The grey woolly monkey moves
comparatively slowly and
carefully through the canopy of
the rain forest, if necessary using
its prehensile tail.*

SWIFT
Callimico goeldii

....

▪ South Colombia, West Brazil,
East Peru, North Bolivia

....

*The small callitrichids like this
spring tamarin move very fast
among the trees, using their claws
instead of the nails that are typical
of primates.*

SELF-CONSCIOUS
Alouatta caraya

▪ South Brazil,
North Argentina, Paraguay

A magnificent male specimen of a black howler monkey, in this case a lighter variation. It is not bothered by the photographer, even though human beings are really the only enemy of this great ape (left).

BELLIGERENT
Alouatta seniculus

▪ Colombia, West Brazil, Peru

This red howler monkey feels disturbed by the photographer and would like to get rid of him—especially since the photographer has just woken it up from a digestive sleep that as a leaf-eater it desperately needs (top right).

SWANKY
Alouatta palliata

▪ Central America, Colombia

A mantled howler monkey doing justice to its name. With its loud singing, this male makes its territorial claim, often supported by other members of the group, (bottom right).

Communication

Why do howler monkeys "howl"?

Often it is very easy to find these shy primates who live concealed in the branches. All you have to do is follow your ears because the groups frequently sing at the top of their voice. In Central America and South America, it is the howler monkeys themselves who inspired their name. In Southeast Asia the songs of the various species of gibbons are famous. And in Madagascar the largest of the lemurs, the indris, greet the new day with a ghostly morning wail. Thus three completely different species of primates have "invented" this form of communication. The chimpanzees, guerezas in Africa and the vari monkeys among the lemurs also do this, although not in so pronounced a manner.

SECURE: When a Guatemala black howler sings it needs to concentrate fully, so it anchors itself with its prehensile tail.

What is this singing all about? Unlike singing birds or humpback whales, in this case the males are not trying to attract females with their tantalizing voices. Always including females, the primates howl to indicate to rival groups that this territory is occupied, in the same as wolf packs howl to mark their territory. In the case of the gibbons the male and female parts are different and so finely in tune with each other that a practiced ear can hear a harmonizing couple. But when you hear a solo singer, it is definitely an invitation to the other sex.

Among the orangutans the males have a so-called "long call." On the one hand this proclaims that the territory is occupied and on the other it may also be call to attract a female wanting to mate—in the same way as humpback whales do. Callitrichids chatter as they look for food, in this way keeping in touch with each other, since it would be all too easy to lose sight of each other in the thick branches. Primates also call each other to warn of danger. In this connection, it has been noticed that among both guenons and New World monkeys the calls are different depending on whether the enemy threat is on the ground or from above. In addition to acoustic communication, a wide range of gestures and facial expressions are used, as they are in the mating season.

AMBITIOUS: The territorial songs of the black and white vari monkeys are not as famous as those of the howler monkeys. Nevertheless this one is doing its best.

Trees are poems that the earth
writes in the sky. We cut them down
and turn them into paper,
to document our emptiness.

KHALIL GIBRAN

WELL-ANCHORED
Ateles paniscus

▪ Guyana, Northeast Brazil

*The prehensile tail is strong enough
to carry the whole weight of the
spider monkey's body. A hand
provides additional security while
the other remains free (right).*

VERY HAIRY
Ateles paniscus

▪ Guyana, Northeast Brazil

*The red-faced spider monkey
does not need a warm furry coat
in the Amazonian rainfores.
Instead it has fairly coarse hair
that allows the frequent rain to
run off easily (bottom left).*

WIDE-NOSED
Ateles chamek

▪ West Brazil, Peru

The distinctive feature of all New World monkeys is the nose: the nostrils face the side instead of the front like all Old World monkeys, including humans. This feature is very evident in this black-faced spider monkey.

ACROBATIC
Ateles geoffroyi

- Central America (Mexico to Colombia)

The Geoffroy spider monkey is an absolute champion climber—partly thanks to its prehensile tail. Leaping is not one of its favorite activities and it cannot swim at all.

Movement

Superfluous like a tail ...

Almost all vertebrates—with the exception of frogs—have a tail. Among the primates, it is not only humans who have divested themselves of a tail in the course of evolution. Our nearest relatives, both the lesser and great apes, are tail-less. This change took place fairly early on in human evolution and it is not at all connected with the fact that we gave up living in trees and became bipeds; orangutans and gibbons for example are never on the ground. There are also tail-less species among the other primates, for instance the Barbary apes of North Africa, the indris of Madagascar and the loris of Asia. Some New World monkeys have not completely divested themselves of this appendage but it is now slightly shorter. Even closely related monkeys can have very different tails: the pig-tailed macaque owes its name to its short crinkly tail. In contrast the Javanese monkeys that share the same habitat (and occasionally even cross-breed) have very long tails.

When tails exist, they are certainly very helpful for climbing monkeys, acting like a balancing pole. Highly-developed tree dwellers therefore often have very long, mobile appendages. Naturally it is brilliant when this tail—as is the case with the South American spider monkey—is also used to hang onto branches. There are several stages in the development of the prehensile tail. Titi monkey couples often sit

DECORATIVE: *The bushy tail of the African guereza monkey and some New World monkeys help them leap from branch to branch.*

together lovingly with their tails entwined. But they cannot hold on with their tails. The prehensile tail of the capuchin monkeys is not yet perfect either. On the other hand, spider monkeys and their relatives have a fully functional fifth hand. Besides being able to hang on to branches with their tails, they are able to use them to grab even the smallest objects.

The monk sakis and guereza monkeys of the African mountain forests clearly demonstrate that a tail is also helpful for other things besides climbing. They have transformed this appendage into very decorative brush and so increased their attractiveness. The lion-tailed macaque of India and the tarsiers have a conspicuous tassel at the end of their tails.

A BRILLIANT TURN: The prehensile tail of the spider monkeys and their relatives further secures their hold on branches and keeps their hands free for other things.

So as colors were created for white,
or women for men, so little animals
were created for mankind.

ELFRIEDE JELINEK

INTELLIGENT
Cebus imitator

▪ Central America (Honduras to Panama)

This Panamanian white-throated capuchin monkey may look a little anxious but of all its relatives it is one of the most intelligent primates. This has repeatedly been demonstrated in tests (bottom left).

RESOURCEFUL
Cebus unicolor

▪ Upper Amazon region

Apparently, this capuchin monkey has found something delicious. Capuchin monkeys do not waste food and they leave little behind if it is edible (bottom right).

A DARK CAP
Sapajus nigritus

▪ Northeast Argentina, Southeast Brazil

Like all representatives of the Sapajus genus, the black capuchin monkey has a cap of dark of hair on its head after which it is named. This individual is still young and later distinctive tufts will grow. This infant is calling for its mother in the Brazilian rain forest (right).

JUMPING POWER
Cebus imitator

▪ Central America (Honduras
to Panama)

*The medium-sized capuchin
monkeys are extremely mobile and
on the move all day long. They look
for food not only in the trees but
often on the ground as well.*

SOCIETY
Cebus imitator

▪ Central America (Honduras to Panama)

Panamanian white-throated capuchin monkeys have been well researched scientifically. Indeed they have been studied since 1923 together with other primates on an island in the Panama Canal.

Reproduction

Becoming a father is not difficult

The "invention" of sexual swelling in female primates is unique in the mammal kingdom. When sexually receptive the genitalia swell conspicuously. A female showing sexual receptiveness is almost irresistible to males. Very different species such as baboons, pig-tailed macaques and chimpanzees have all developed this feature independently of each other. They all live in troops with several males of which only the highest-ranking members will mate. In the case of the gorillas only the pasha of the harem has the right to mate with the sexually receptive females. But it sometimes happens that one of its ladies decides to "enjoy" herself with a younger male and the "boss" generously puts up with this.

With most primates it is exclusively the mother that looks after the young. This is why it is all the more surprising to see the male silver back gorilla playing with its young. In the case of chimpanzees it has been observed that males have adopted an infant when the baby's mother has died.

Extremely unusual—and almost unique among mammals—is the rearing of the young among callitrichids. Immediately after birth the father takes over the young—almost always twins—and carries them around. When the babies are hungry the father

EMANCIPATION: In the case of pygmy marmosets, the father and other members of the group take it in turns to carry the young.

dutifully hands them over to the mother to suckle. But otherwise the father is the perfect babysitter, carrying the babies around on its back most of the time. Often the older children help in this task, carrying their siblings around from time to time.

It is typical of the greater primates that the babies are carried by the mother for a certain time—in anthropoid apes this can be a whole year. Some of the prosimians actually leave their young in the nest while they go out looking for food. Clinging young or nestlings—another interesting difference between prosimian and simians.

PACK ANIMAL: With callitrichids the birth of twins is the rule, as is the fact that the tamarin father carries the children.

A FINE MOUSTACHE
Saguinus imperator

▪ West Brazil, Southeast Peru, Northwest Bolivia

Several primates have beards or moustaches. But the male emperor tamarin exceeds all others in length—in this case quite literally. Even the moustache of Kaiser Wilhelm II, in whose honor he was named, was no more impressive although perhaps it was more artistically curled.

READY TO JUMP
Saguinus tripartitus

▪ Northeast Ecuador, North Peru

The golden-mantle saddleback tamarin is still holding on with its hands but its tensed rear legs are about to catapult it into the next tree in a single bound.

NAKED EARS
Mico argentatus

- Northeast Brazil

Its large ears, naked and flesh-colored, enable the silvery marmoset to hear particularly well. They are the conspicuously distinctive characteristic of the species.

BRUSH EARS
Callithrix jacchus

▪ Northeast Brazil

Many callitrichids have brush-like tufts of hair on their ears. Those of the common marmoset are particularly elegant and impressive.

Lion tamarins can be really aggressive. They then bristle their mane, show their teeth, shriek very loudly in shrill tones and bite very powerfully.

HERBERT WENDT

PERFECTLY HEALTHY
Cacajao calvus

 West Brazil, East Peru

To us this monkey with its bald head and red face does not look well. But in the case of the bald uakari both these features are signs of glowing health (top left).

BLOND HAIR
Cacajao calvus

▪ West Brazil, East Peru

The light-colored variation of the red uakari belongs to the same species as the red-haired ones and like them it has a tail that is 8 inches (20 cm) long at the most (bottom left).

FOUR-HANDED
Cacajao calvus

▪ West Brazil, East Peru

All monkeys—not only these uakaris—have hands and feet that are extremely sensitive and capable of picking up the smallest objects with great precision. In fact, the term "handed animals" would be applicable to the entire mammal genus (right).

No other monkey looks as much like a child as the titi monkey; it has the same expression of innocence, the same arch smile, the same quick transition from delight to tearfulness.

ALEXANDER VON HUMBOLDT

EXTRAVAGANT
Chiropotes sagulatus

▪ Guyana, North Brazil

The male Guyana red-backed bearded saki has an impressively thick beard and a magnificent decorative double cowl. The bushy tail further adds to the imposing appearance of the only medium-sized monkey (right).

FRUGAL
Callicebus brunneus

▪ West Brazil, East Peru

The titi has only recently become the subject of serious research and as result it has been divided into over thirty different species. The brown titi of the upper reaches of the Amazon is considered hardly endangered (bottom left).

WHITE HEAD
Saguinus oedipus

▪ Colombia

The Liszt monkey, named after the composer Franz Liszt because of its shock of white hair, is seriously endangered because of the destruction of its habitat.

RED HANDS
Saguinus midas

▪ Guyana, North Brazil

The head and body of this golden handed tamarin are rather inconspicuous but the striking color of its hands and feet distinguishes the species.

PALE HANDS
Saguinus leucopus

▪ Kolumbien

This white-footed tamarin ventures as far as the suburbs—they are not as threatened as the Liszt monkeys in Colombia.

The monkey is a monster in
his carnal love but in his moral
love he could show many
people how to behave!

ALFRED BREHM

WELL-PROTECTED
Saimiri boliviensis

....

▪ West Brazil, Peru, Bolivia

....

The black-capped squirrel monkeys live in groups of more than sixty individuals. They are too small to be hunted and have many protected habitats so that they are not an endangered species (bottom left).

WHITE LIPS
Saguinus labiatus

....

▪ West Brazil, Peru, Bolivien

....

Also known as the red-bellied tamarin, the mouth area of the white-lipped tamarin is even more striking than the red chest and belly region of this monkey, because it looks as if it had been painted white. They are very widespread and not yet endangered (bottom right).

BLACK HEAD
Leontopithecus caissara

....

▪ Southeast Brazil

....

The habitat of the black-faced lion tamarin is less than 115 square miles (300 square kilometers) and they number about 400 individuals. They are therefore seriously endangered (right)-

Those who really know a dog
or monkey, or a higher mammal,
and are still not convinced
that these creatures have
feelings like themselves, are
emotionally abnormal.

KONRAD LORENZ

▪ East Venezuela and Guyana
to North Brazil

*Including its magnificent tail,
the white-faced saki is three feet
(almost one meter) long, so it is
not particularly small. Its hands
are extremely soft (bottom left).
The males are black with a white
face while the mottled grey females
only have white stripes round
the mouth area. In spite of this
big gender difference, they do not
live in harems but in small mixed
groups (right).*

Old World monkeys

BEAUTIFUL FRIENDS: *The black snub-nosed monkeys that are only found in a remote corner of China and in Tibet have rarely been photographed up to now.*

Old World monkeys

Successful in all situations

A surprising encounter in the mountains of Ethiopia—a large troop of monkeys is on the move on the bare grassy plains without any trees as far as the eye can see. Even in these extremely harsh surroundings they seem to be doing very well.

The geleda baboons do not correspond at all to the mental picture that one has of a monkey. They are rarely seen in trees. They sleep on rocky cliffs and at vertiginous heights of over 13,000 feet (4,000 meters). Extraordinary—but then little is "normal" with Old World monkeys!

With over 150 species and wide-ranging physical differences, Old World monkeys are the most diverse and adaptable of all primates. They live in the rain forests of Africa and Asia as well as in the mountains of Japan, China and Ethiopia. They are found in the Arabian peninsula and on the Rock of Gibraltar. They also feel at home in Indian mega-cities as well as in the uninhabited savanna on the edge of the Sahara. With the exception of deserts, there is no habitat that these jacks of all trades have not conquered.

At first glance the Old World monkeys differ from the New World monkeys of South America (to which in a wider sense the great apes also belong) in their narrow nasal septum. This means that their nostrils face towards the front and not towards the side. They are widespread in Africa south of the Sahara as well in southern Asia from Pakistan to the islands of Indonesia and the Philippines. Two of the species live relatively far from the main area of distribution: the Japanese red-faced macaque and the Barbary monkeys—which are also macaques—that live in the Atlas mountains and on Gibraltar, which means also in Europe.

There are also a few "purists" that feed entirely on leaves.

As far as food is concerned, their taste varies enormously. On one hand, there are large numbers of omnivores which feed on fruit, seeds and buds but will not scorn bird's eggs, insects and even young antelopes. In Africa these "generalist" omnivores include baboons, guenons and mangabeys, and in Asia macaques. Many of them have cheek pouches that they soon cram full with

> **The mangabeys do not have the cheerful liveliness and irrepressible frivolity that are the famous characteristics of guenons.**
>
> ALFRED BREHM

GROUND-FORAGING: The red-capped mangabey, with a habitat from Nigeria to Gabon, prefers looking for food on the ground.

their favorite foods. They then withdraw to a safer place where they can quietly eat all the food stuffed in their cheeks. On the other hand, there are also a few "purists" that feed entirely on leaves. These include the African colobus or guerezas and the Asian leaf monkeys, ranging from the various langurs to the exquisite proboscis monkeys, douc langurs and snub-nosed monkeys. To cope with their indigestible, although plentifully available, diet of leaves and buds, like ruminants they have developed specially adapted stomachs that enables them to digest the cellulose of leaves.

Because of this unusual diet these leaf-eaters (or folivores) are rarely found in zoos. The commonest monkeys living in zoos are the relatively robust African guerezas or Indian hanuman langurs. The proboscis and douc langurs, which were still being bred in the Frankfurt and Cologne zoos in the 1970s, to the great pride of the zoo authorities, have now disappeared from captivity. The reason for this is that in the long term the very varied leaf diet of their tropical forests cannot be exactly reproduced or replaced in a zoo. By contrast, monkeys familiar to zoo

> **Our aversion to monkeys is caused both by their physical and their intellectual abilities. They look too much and at the same time too little like humans.**
>
> ALFRED BREHM

LOVINGLY: Social grooming, here of a female hussar monkey by a male, is not only a matter of mutual cleaning. Among primates it also plays an important part in ensuring the cohesion of the group.

visitors are the robust macaques, with the rhesus monkeys leading the way (these were also used in laboratories, and to them we owe the discovery of the rhesus factor in blood) as well as the baboons.

The social life of Old World monkeys is also very different. Most of them live in troops with a strict hierarchy. Among forest dwellers comparatively small family groups still exist; otherwise it would be all too easy for them to lose sight of each other. By contrast, the troops of baboons living in open habitat, for instance savannahs, sometimes include several hundred individuals. In the case of the gelada baboon, groups of over 600 individuals have been sighted. And among the snub-nosed monkeys of China,

similarly large groups have been observed. The troops of hamadryas baboons are not much smaller.

A particular strong male gathers a bevy of ladies around it.

Like the mandrills and drills living in the central African rain forest, the proboscis monkey of Borneo and a number of species of langur, they have developed a harem structure. A particular strong male—in the case of the hamadryas baboon, clearly identified by its magnificent mane, and in the case of the proboscis monkey

by its striking pendulous nose—gathers a bevy of ladies around it. If in the evening several harem groups find themselves together on their favorite "sleeping rocks" (where they feel protected from leopards prowling at night), no lady is allowed to move away from her "owner." In monkey societies where the males are considerably larger than the females or differ conspicuously in appearance from them, as is the case with proboscis monkeys or mandrills, one can observe that there is such harem structure. A peculiarity of a number of Old World monkeys living in large groups with several males or in harem groups is the genital swelling of the females, which magically attract admirers when they are fertile. The classification of Old World monkeys is as extensive as their habitats, diet and social life. In the past the guenon-like monkeys and the highly specialized langurs, also known as leaf monkeys, were classed separately because of the latter's leaf diet. Today they have all been classified in the Cercopithecidae family, from the macaques and baboons to the proboscis monkeys and doucs. But instead of a small number of species there are now an impressive two dozen. Of all these species, the ones that are most endangered are those that live in forests in relatively small habitats. These include the proboscis monkeys in Borneo, the doucs in Vietnam and the snub-nosed monkeys in China, and more especially the pig-tailed snub-nosed monkeys that only live on the Mentawai islands to the west of Sumatra.

AGGRESSIVE: The Assam
macaque, a close relative of
the equally aggressive rhesus
monkey, clearly shows that it
is ready to fight.

Africa is home not only to the largest, the cleverest and the most hateful Old World monkeys but also to the most beautiful, likeable and good-natured ones.

ALFRED BREHM

WHITE-BEARDED
Allochrocebus solatus

▪ Gabon

The Gabon sun-tailed monkey was not discovered until 1984. It is only found in a small area and as a result it has been declared the nature preservation "flagship species" in its country (right).

WHITE-LIPPED
Cercopithecus cephus

▪ Central Africa (South Cameroun, Gabon to North Angola)

While it is called the moustached guenon, the white stripe above the upper lip is even more conspicuous. It is very visible, as is typical of primates with striking eyes (bottom left).

WHITE-THROATED
Cercopithecus albogularis

▪ East to South Africa, Zanzibar

The widespread white-throated guenon is rather inconspicuous and unobtrusive in appearance. It avoids standing out at all costs and is hard to see in the jungle (bottom right).

CENTRAL
Cercopithecus ascanius

▪ Democratic Republic of the Congo to North Angola

The red-tailed guenon monkey is widespread in the Congo rain forest, stretching as far as Uganda to the east and to Angola in the south (left top).

EXQUISITE
Cercopithecus kandti

▪ Ruanda, East Congo, South West Uganda

The golden guenon monkey only occurs in a very small area of the Central African Rift Valley and it is therefore considered endangered (left bottom).

FAR WEST
Cercopithecus roloway

▪ Ghana, Ivory Coast

Of all the monkeys shown here, the roloway guenon with its striking black and white coat occurs the furthest west, as far as the Ivory Coast (bottom left).

EXTERNAL
Cercopithecus albogularis

▪ East to South Africa

The majority of the guenon monkeys live in the rain forest of West and Central Africa. But the habitat of the white-throated guenon monkey is the East Coast from Kenya as far as South Africa (bottom right).

UNUSUAL
Chlorocebus djamdjamensis

▪ West Ethiopia

The Bale Mountains vervet lives in regions above 8,000 to 10,000 feet (2,400 to 3,000 meters), in other words at very high altitudes. Its diet is also very unusual for guenons: the soft inner pith of bamboos but also the young leaves. Another striking feature is its blue scrotum. All Bale Mountains vervet monkeys have this very visible attribute of their maleness.

Color

The colorful world of monkeys

The colorful and gorgeous mask of the mandrill is a really striking feature. The blue triangle in the face of the Asian snub-nosed monkey is equally striking. The scrotum of the green guenon monkey and the lips of the moustached guenon are also extremely colorful. Equally striking are the bright red lips and gums of the gelada baboon as are the red genital swelling with which some female primates attract their men. No other mammal can boast such colorfulness; in fact it would quite wasted on them because, for instance, hoofed animals cannot see the color red.

Apart from most prosimians and South American owl monkeys, primates have developed diurnal visual creatures. Visual creatures are creatures that are guided mainly by their visual skills. The magnificent colors of the primates' fur and body parts are used to communicate. Even so the color vision of primates is still in the early stages of infancy, as indeed is ours. Our perception of color is nowhere near as sophisticated as the perception of color by birds, insects or reptiles. With the exception of the color red that plays an important part in sexual matters, for instance, we ourselves have not developed our own body colors. So we add lipstick and eye shadow as well as colorful clothes.

The gloriously colorful mandrills probably played a pioneering role in the history of evolution. The pri-

BEAUTY: *The golden snub-nosed monkeys in China are among the most colorful of all primates.*

mates may have been on the way to becoming as colorful as butterflies. But this is not true of all of them. Color is useless in the case of nocturnal animals, which is why owl monkeys have a black and white pattern. Many of the Madagascar lemurs have this contrasting fur. This is true even of the few of them that have become completely diurnal, such as the ring-tailed lemurs and the white sifaka. In their case appearance has not kept up with their lifestyle—so far they have not been able to remove their black and white pajamas.

Only one color is still completely underdeveloped in primates. Unlike insects or reptiles, so far there is no green. So human punks with green hair are far ahead of evolution.

DETERRENT: *the colorful mask of the male mandrill is already impressive enough but the bared canine teeth cannot fail to inspire respect as well.*

THREATENING
Mandrillus sphinx

▪ South Cameroun, Guinea, Gabon

Not even a leopard has canines as enormous as this mandrill. No one would dare get into a fight with it. Among males the threat alone is usually enough (left).

ON THE TREE
Mandrillus sphinx

▪ South Cameroun, Guinea, Gabon

The relatively small female mandrill with its young likes climbing high up in the trees in search of food. There it is safe from possible enemies (top right).

ON THE GROUND
Mandrillus sphinx

▪ South Cameroun, Guinea, Gabon

Male mandrills are the largest of all the "lower" apes. Weighing up to 45 to 65 pounds (20 to 30 kilograms), they are three times as heavy as the females. The males prefer to stay on the ground. Both sexes are colorful (bottom right).

MASK-LIKE
Mandrillus leucophaeus

▪ Southeast Nigeria,
West Cameroun

Not quite as large and colorful as the mandrill is its close relative, the drill. Instead of a colorful mask, it has one like polished ebony. Both the mandrill and the drill have a similar lifestyle: they live in very large troopss of several males and twice as many females, led by a dominant male. The drill is an endangered species.

CHALLENGING
Mandrillus leucophaeus

▪ Southeast Nigeria,
West Cameroun

Why drills are so powerful and striking is a question that has been debated for a long time. Because they do not have an actual harem, the respect their size inspires tends to prevent fights among males. A threatening look is enough (left).

FAVORITE LADIES
Theropithecus gelada

▪ Ethiopia

A male gelada baboon can weigh as much as 65 pounds (30 kilograms) while the females in the harem are only half that. The females only carry their infants against their breast for the first three weeks, then they carry them on their backs. The young are breast-fed for a long time, for a good year in fact (bottom right).

I deliberately chose the rainy season to go and visit the gelada baboons in Simien National Park in Ethiopia. In these conditions light is more diffuse, and without sunlight contrasts are less strong. The surroundings were a lush green and there were no tourists. It was so impressive to sit there in the middle of hundred of baboons. Often it was very misty, and one day a magnificent male with a beautiful mane suddenly appeared through the mist! Another day I became frightened when I suddenly noticed hundreds of animals shrieking in my direction. It turned out that I was not the reason for this, the cause being an enormous bird of prey in the sky. Baby gelada baboons often fall prey to flying predators.

THOMAS MARENT

PLAYFUL CHILDREN
Theropithecus gelada

▪ Ethiopia

Everyone knows that young animals love playing; we know this from kittens, puppies and foals. But as far as the joy of playing is concerned young primates beat all other animal babies hands down. These gelada baboons in the sparse mountain forests of Ethiopia are no exception. There is much running, shouting and playful mounting, in other words practicing for the emergencies of life (left and right).

FAMILY PHOTOGRAPH
Theropithecus gelada

▪ Ethiopia

The gelada pasha sits proudly with his ladies. He has appropriated as many as a dozen to himself, often after bloody fights with rivals. Only then can he perform his main duty, that of ensuring the next generation. He too has the red mark on his chest (118-119).

GRAZERS
Theropithecus gelada

▪ Ethiopia

The gelada baboons spend more time on the ground than any other monkey. Their parsimonious diet in habitats at altitudes of up to 14,500 feet (4,400 meters) consists mostly of grasses, which even the magnificent male in the foreground appears to enjoy (left).

SUPERMAN
Theropithecus gelada

▪ Ethiopia

Male geladas are among the most impressive primates. They are not only twice as big as the females but they also have handsome manes on their head and shoulders— perfect for attracting a harem. But the competition is fierce and other males are equally beautiful (bottom right).

> **About who created the world is debatable. Sure is who destroys the world.**
>
> GEORGE ADAMSON

WHIPPERSNAPPERS
Papio anubis

▪ West to East Africa

It will be a few years before this young Anubis baboon has fought his way up in the hierarchy of his group. But he is already working at it (top left).

FOND OF CHILDREN
Papio anubis

▪ Westto East Africa

Newly-born Anubis baboons still have the dark, almost black baby fur that attracts the attention of all the members of the group, especially those who have never had babies before (bottom left).

A REAL MAN
Papio hamadryas

▪ Southwest Arabia, Northeast Africa

The hamadryas baboon is the baboon species that has a real harem structure: a magnificent male with an impressive mane has won the favors of up to nine wives whom he defends not only by threats but also by using his teeth against his rivals if necessary (top right).

CHILD ORIENTED
Papio hamadryas

▪ Southwest Arabia, Northeast Africa

The baby hamadryas baboon still has its baby fur but it will not be breast-fed for much longer so that it will soon make short reconnaissance forays (bottom right).

FOND OF FLOWERS
Macaca nigra

....

▪ North Sulawesi

....

Like all the other macaques, the black macaques are omnivores. Two thirds of their food consist of fruits of all kind but they also appreciate insects and other animal flesh. Here this male is trying an Amorphophallus, part of the arum family. Of the seven endemic macaque species on the island of Sulawesi, this is the most threatened species.

It was a fascinating experience for me to accompany a group of black macaques in the Tangkoko Reserve in Sulawesi. They were so used to people that I did not have to wear the same T-shirt for four consecutive days, as had once happened to a nature photographer. One day the monkeys came upon a wonderful Amorphophallus plant and decided to inspect one of its giant flowers at close range. Naturally, this was a unique opportunity for me to take a fantastic photograph.

THOMAS MARENT

All members of the monkey genus displays a striking affection and love for their young.

PLINY THE ELDER

CUDDLY
Macaca sylvanus

▪ Morocco, Algeria, Gibraltar

Barbary apes in the Atlas Mountains of North Africa and in Gibraltar must cope with the cold. So it is good to be able to huddle together for warmth with the baby in the middle. Numbering less than 7,000 in the wild, Barbary apes are considered threatened (right).

CHILDLIKE
Macaca sylvanus

▪ Morocco, Algeria, Gibraltar

At birth, the coat of many infant primates is often quite a different color from that of their parents. This explains why this little Barbary macaque will lose its black cap after just a few weeks (bottom left).

POWERFUL
Macaca nemestrina

▪ Thailand, Malaysia, Sumatra, Borneo

Macaques are quite strong. The males of the southern pig-tailed macaques are almost twice as large as the females. Because of their strength, they are often tamed when young and trained to harvest coconuts (bottom right).

Habitats

Not all of them sit in trees

Primates in the snow and on the ice, are there such things? The popular belief is that monkeys live in tropical forests. But not all do: rhesus monkeys and Tibet macaques live in the Himalayas and Japanese macaques live in icy conditions, and the Ethiopian gelada baboons live on tree-less grasslands at altitudes of up to 16,000 feet (5,000 meters).

The hussar monkeys that are part of the guenon family have also left the forest and live in the grass savannah to the north of the Congo rain forest. In order to adapt to this almost tree-less habitat they have developed particularly long arms and legs—they are the greyhounds of the monkey world. The green guenon monkeys have not gone quite that far, living in the tree savannah of eastern and southern Africa. They often climb thorn trees to gather the flowers and fruits.

All baboon species live predominantly on the ground, including the mandrills and drills living in the Central African rainforest. As a result they have the most varied diet, being omnivores, as are chimpanzees. The gorillas live almost entirely on the ground. Climbing up a tree is far from easy or safe for a silverback male weighing 440 pounds (200 kilograms).

The Asian great apes that hardly ever leave their trees behave quite differently. Although weighing almost 220 pounds (100 kilograms), the orangutan swings nonchalantly through the canopy with great

HIGH UP: Gold snub-nosed monkeys live in tree-less habitats at altitudes of up to 10,000 feet (3,000 meters), so lichen is on the menu.

agility using his long arms. They always build their nests high up in the trees. Gibbons are even more highly developed tree dwellers, moving from tree top to tree top with incredible nimbleness.

The African guereza and the Asian langurs that feed only on leaves live exclusively in the forest. The New World monkeys have a similar lifestyle and diet. They have remained forest dwellers. Among the prosimians only the ring-tailed lemurs can be found regularly on the ground while the white sifakas "dance" over open spaces with breathtaking leaps.

A COLD ISLAND: Japanese macaques live in a region that is on the same latitude as New York so they too have a lot of snow.

I was happy when on the fourth day of my stay with the Japanese macaques a snow storm suddenly broke out because these animals have become very popular with photographers. The monkeys sitting in the hot springs were indeed an amazing sight but everyone knows these pictures. Now at last I could take pictures of monkeys in a snow storm and show the harsh conditions in which these macaques live. But after a few hours the camera iced up and I could no longer see through the viewfinder. So I just pointed the camera in the direction of the monkeys, tried to choose the right detail and pressed the button.

THOMAS MARENT

THICK FUR
Macaca fuscata

▪ Japan

You can see how thick the fur of Japanese macaques is from the fact that the snow that has accumulated on it does not melt. Fur is a prerequisite for surviving in these harsh conditions (right).

TOGETHERNESS
Macaca fuscata

▪ Japan

JJapanese macaques are used to the cold.Even so it easier to survive it when sitting together because they can keep each other nice and warm. Their red faces have nothing to do with the sub-zero temperatures but are typical of this species (bottom left).

BEAUTIFULLY CLOSE
Macaca fuscata

• Japan

*Solidarity is the rule among
primates. Japanese macaques,
also known as snow monkeys, are
rarely aggressive and they have
many social interactions. Huddling
together is vitally important in
the extreme conditions of winter
in northern Japan. At the same
time the younger of the two baby
monkeys is still suckling.*

BEAUTIFULLY WARM
Macaca fuscata

▪ Japan

The snow monkeys of Nagano province have become famous because on cold winter days they spend hours in hot springs. However, only groups of monkeys at the top of the hierarchy have access. The others have to wait in the cold out of the water.

To us monkeys are a caricature of man
and amuse us as long as they show us
their good side: but as soon as they
reveal their bad side, we condemn
them to damnation.

ALFRED BREHM

PARADISE
Macaca nemestrina

• Thailand, Malaysia, Sumatra, Borneo

The southern pig-tailed macaques live in the tropical forests of Southeast Asia as people generally imagine primates live. But even in paradise things are not always peaceful, for instance when this male becomes threatening (bottom left).

SPOILT
Macaca silenus

• Southwest India

This lion-tail macaque or wanderoo has plenty of food at its disposal. The good thing about figs is that they do not all ripen at the same time so they provide food for months on end. But many creatures like them and eventually the harvest comes to an end. The lion-tail macaque is an endangered species because its habitat is shrinking (right).

WELL PROTECTED
Macaca radiata

• South India

The Indian bonnet macaque and its relatives in Sri Lanka have the most elegant hair-dos of all macaques. Apart from this they are very similar to the rhesus monkeys that are widespread throughout south-east Asia. Perhaps the thatch of hair helps to avoid possible "intermarriages" (136-137).

PATIENCE
Macaca assamensis

▪ China, Assam, Myanmar,
Laos, Vietnam, North and
West Thailand

*The little Assam macaque would
much prefer to go off with its mates
and play. But the mother desides
that it is time for social grooming.
This is how she keeps her child
clean and free of parasites.*

SUSPENSE
Macaca fascicularis

▪ Southeast Asia: Cambodia to Philippines, Java and Bali

Apparently this Javanese monkey has discovered something very exciting. But in the next minute it will probably move quickly to safety. These macaques are widespread throughout the southeastern mainland but also on the islands, such as this individual. in the Philippines. Everywhere they look a little different.

FRUGAL
Piliocolobus kirkii

▪ Zanzibar

It is obvious that the Zanzibar colobus loves to eat leaves more than anything else, and there are plenty of leaves on Zanzibar. But this diet requires a special gastro-intestinal system to digest this food, as well as a lot of time. Happily these beautiful monkeys have plenty of that.

CONTRASTING
Colobus guereza

▪ South Cameroun to Kenya and Ethiopia

Guereza monkeys are completely monochrome, depending entirely on the combination of black and white. As well as the white frame round their face and a more or less white tail, depending on the subspecies, they also have white fringes running from the shoulders down to the rump. The Kilimanjaro subspecies has even more white fur than this Mount Kenya subspecies (left).

A DIFFERENT COLOR
Colobus guereza

▪ South Cameroun to Kenya and Ethiopia

Guereza babies are born completely white and start changing color at about three to four weeks. When they are six months old, this process is complete. The striking white fur that many new langur babies have ensures that the baby receives a lot of care and attention, and not only from its mother (right).

INSULAR
Piliocolobus kirkii

▪ Zanzibar

There are eighteen species of red colobus monkeys from Sierra Leone to East Africa, each one occupying a relatively small area. But the habitat of the Zanzibar colobus extends to just over 400 square miles (1,000 square kilometers); they often roam on the edge of villages. Being leaf eaters they cause hardly any problems and are tolerated even in mango trees. Yet this species is endangered (144-145).

Presbytis thomasi

....

▪ North Sumatra

....

This little Thomas langur must be a few months old because it has already lost all its white baby fur. In the case of a female it will be sexually mature at the age of five and will be carried off by a male for its harem (left).

CHILDLIKE
Trachypithecus obscurus

....

▪ South Thailand, South Myanmar, Malaysia

....

With their gold-colored fur, young spectacled langurs are among the most appealing animal babies—and not only among primates. Their cuteness is such that all the members of the group want to be allowed to mother the baby (bottom right).

Like good Hindus, langurs have a relatively strict vegetarian diet.

VOLKER SOMMER

> **Apart from their impertinence,
> these monkeys (Hanuman langurs)
> are smart and attractive creatures.**
>
> ALFRED BREHM

The maroon langur that is widespread on the island of Borneo was described scientifically for the first time over 100 years before its "cute" relative on the mainland. Because it finds food in second-growth forests and also in plantations it is not considered endangered (right).

It hard to believe that this striking golden langur was only discovered in 1956. But the foothills of the Himalayas in Assam and Bhutan where it is found had never been explored by scientists before and therefore never researched. Only 5,000 in number, this species is naturally endangered (bottom left).

Genealogical relationships

Holy and unholy monkeys

The attitude of human beings to their relatives is very ambivalent. In ancient Egypt baboons were worshipped as gods and embalmed after their death. And in India monkeys are still seen as holy creatures—not the rhesus monkey, which is considered vermin, but the harmless, leaf-eating grey langur. They are dedicated to the god Hanuman and play an important part in the Hindu epic *Ramayana*. Their black hands and faces reflect their attempts to save Princess Sita, who had been carried off by a demon; their hands and face were charred in the fire that had been lit to rescue the princess. Many Indian temples are adorned with statues of the monkey god and on his feast day believers bring the langurs food.

But there are no langurs on the island of Bali, which is also Hindu. So there people worship and feed the Javanese monkeys, the main protagonists in the famous Kecak monkey dance. In Thailand, temple monkeys are not only tolerated but spoilt with goodies. And in Japan no one would ever lay a hand on a macaque. The Dayaks in Borneo keep the skulls of orangutans as they do those of people.

But things are very different in Africa and South America. In those countries there is no respect or veneration for our closest relatives. In fact, monkeys played an important part in the diet of Indians and pygmies. Even today gorillas and chimpanzees are

UNAPPRECIATED: *Gold langurs are not seen as holy. Although endangered, they are still hunted today.*

still on the menu. Madagascar is an exception. It is true that when the first people arrived on the island some 2,000 years ago, they hunted lemurs and exterminated the biggest species. But that is now largely in the past. One species has always been taboo: no one would dare to come too close to an aye-aye or to kill it.

In European civilizations monkeys have long been demonized or ridiculed. Since the 12th century monkeys have accompanied acrobats and jugglers as "jesters." Unfortunately not much has changed in this attitude. In television series chimpanzees are still represented as badly behaved children. Respect is something else.

VENERABLE: *Of all the primates, India's Hanuman langurs are the most treasured, being considered holy by devout Hindus.*

SERIOUSLY ENDANGERED
Trachypithecus leucocephalus

▪ Southern China

More than a dozen white-headed langurs in a single photograph — this is quite remarkable in view of the fact that the overall population is only just over 600. It is gratifying to see that evidently every female has a child, from the gold-colored baby to the whitish teenagers. Leaves make up 90 percent of the diet of these white-headed langurs, here seen clinging to the karst rocks.

**People in Senegal
firmly believe that monkeys
are people like us but
cleverer because they have
refrained from learning to speak
in order not to be
recognized as people and
be forced to work.** HEINRICH HEINE

CONTRASTING
Trachypithecus cristatus)

▪ Sumatra, Borneo

Mother and child could be hardly be more different in colour than these two silvered langurs. But even when the golden-coloured youngster has reached adulthood, its colour can range from pale grey to almost black. These leaf-eaters are threatened by the clearing of their forests in favour of palm oil plantations (left).

GREYHEAD
Trachypithecus pileatus

▪ Northeast India, Bangladesh

All capped langurs have a grey cap—otherwise the color of their fur varies. As usual for most langurs, the groups are led by a single male. He must watch his rivals very carefully and when resting usually he sits with his penis erect and clearly visible (bottom right).

▪ Borneo

The nose of the male proboscis monkey is much larger than that of the female and also than that of other primates. The males love to flaunt their sexual organ—here even when jumping (left).

THIRSTY
Nasalis larvatus

▪ Borneo

Two generic features of this proboscis monkey get in the way when he has to drink, his long nose and his large belly. The belly of the proboscis monkey is twice as large as that of other langurs—an excellent adjustment for eating leaves. The animals never live far from the water (bottom right).

Already 20 years ago I wanted to take pictures of the proboscis monkeys living in the mangrove forests of Borneo. Unfortunately the results were rather disappointing because the animals were just too shy. Ten years later, when I visited the National Park again, the situation had considerably improved for me. The reason was that the monkeys had become used to people. They allowed me to photograph them and I was able to take some amazing pictures of animals in the mangrove swamps. At low tide they made their way to the mangroves to find their favorite food, the leaves of mangrove trees.

THOMAS MARENT

> **Wherever an animal is forced into the service of man, the pain it experiences concerns us all.**
>
> ALBERT SCHWEITZER

EXTRAVAGANT
Pygathrix nemaeus

▪ Laos, North Vietnam, Northeast Cambodia

In appearance this douc (here the red-shanked douc) surpasses all other primates as far as colorfulness and elegance is concerned. And this male seems to be very aware of his gorgeous looks (right).

VERY FEMININE
Nasalis larvatus

▪ Borneo

The female proboscis monkeys have a girlish snub nose. They are also considerably smaller than the males and their belly is not quite as large. As this great gender difference suggests, these monkeys live in harem groups with up to nine females for one male (bottom left).

ADMIRABLE
Rhinopithecus bieti

▪ Southwest China,
Southeast Tibet

The black snub-nosed monkey live in the evergreen mountain forests with spruces, larches and cypresses as well as in bamboo thickets at altitudes of between 10,000 and 15,500 feet (3,000 to 4,700 meters)—higher than any other non-human primate.

VERY ENDANGERED
Rhinopithecus bieti

▪ Southwest China,
Southeast Tibet

*In 2006 the number of these
beautiful monkeys was estimated
at about 2,000 individuals. The
reason for this low number is their
dwindling habitat. In addition,
many of them die in snares set to
catch musk deer, the glandular
secretions of which are used
in medicine.*

TENURE
Rhinopithecus roxellana

▪ West and Central China

The impressive male golden snub-nosed monkey usually leads a harem of twenty to thirty individuals. This one appears to have discovered a rival and he is clearly signaling that he had better stay away. Even so, several harems often merge together to form groups of between 200 to 600 individuals. They are the most common of the five snub-nosed species but even so they are endangered.

GUTSY YOUNG
Rhinopithecus roxellana

▪ West and Central China

This young golden snub-nosed monkey that has just started changing into its adult color, is leaping among the rocks. These monkeys in central China live in the harshest habitat of all primates: conifer forests, rhododendron and bamboo thickets at altitudes of up to 10,000 feet (3,000 meters).

A SWANKY MALE
Rhinopithecus roxellana

▪ West and Central China

It is not only their color but also their size that make these monkeys some of the most impressive primates. This is especially true of the male which can weigh up to 90 pounds (40 kilograms).

THICK FUR
Rhinopithecus roxellana

▪ West and Central China

The winters in the mountains in China can be extremely cold and snowy. This is why couples normally keep each other warm or mothers keep their babies warm between their bodies. So it is all the more surprising that this young animal is sitting completely alone. Fortunately, like all golden snub-nosed monkeys it has thick fur to protect it in winter. Its food in that season is quite basic: it consists only of spruce needles, lichen and tree bark (left and right).

Great apes

VERY CLEVER: The orangutan mother in the Tanjung Puting National Park protects herself and her young from the rain with an umbrella made of leaves.

Our closest relatives

Encountering chimpanzees and gorilla in the wild is simply breathtaking. And not only because of the physical effort that is needed to do so.

Anyone who is able to observe the family life of our closest relatives, the mothers with their babies, the children laughing and romping around, the patient silverback male with a half-grown child climbing on its back, will immediately notice this incredible close relationship. Apart from size, of course, because compared to a 450-pound (200-kilogram) gorilla we are very small. No, we feel it: they are exactly like us. Much closer than we had previously thought. Anyone who has been fortunately enough to see a chimpanzee looking for termites with a tool they have made themselves will become even more aware of this close relationship—so different and yet so similar.

Until recently man and the family of Hominidae were grouped with the great and lower apes. They were the "summit of creation." Linnaeus had already referred to this with the name Primates designating this whole class of mammals. Nothing has changed here. But the division of the hominoids valid until now has been altered.

Because of recent genetic findings the special position of man has come to an end. Man is now in the same family as the chimpanzees, gorillas and orangutans. Slightly apart but not far away are the small apes, the gibbons.

These separated from the human family tree some 20 million years ago. They were followed considerably later by the orangutans, then by the gorillas. On the other hand, the chimpanzees and humans only went their separate ways five to eight million years ago. The surprising result is that chimpanzees are more closely related to us than to gorillas.

> *Chimpanzees and humans only went their separate ways five to eight million years ago.*

The genetic difference is only two percent (to be exact, 1.37 percent according to the most recent findings)! Hence the new classification.

The differences between humans and Old World monkeys are relatively small. Even the most striking feature is not unique: some Old World monkeys (and even prosimians) have also reduced the length of their tail. The head is relatively round, the nose

PENSIVE: Even without communicating with it, we can understand the expression in the eyes of this young chimpanzee.

or snout area is short and the forehead is relatively large. Compared to the all other primates the arms of the great apes are very long.

This feature is particularly pronounced in the case of the gibbons, which perfectly developed their way of moving hand over hand, in other words, swinging from branch to branch. The difference in length between arms and legs is less pronounced in orangutans. Because of their much greater weight they do not swing with only their arms but they also use their legs for extra safety. In the case of chimpanzees and gorillas the arms are not particularly long. All hominoids have a broader thorax, a spinal column that is more in the centre and an elongated collarbone, as well as stronger hands that are better adapted to manipulation.

Pregnancy is relatively long for our closest relatives, ranging from seven months (for gibbons) to nine months. Very rarely (most frequently among humans) twins are born. The children are looked after by the mother for a comparatively long time: a minimum of two years and quite often up to four to six years. All anthropoid apes arrive at adulthood quite late, with the gibbons reaching maturity the youngest, at between six to eight years; in the case of their large relatives— orangutans, gorillas and chimpanzees—it is even later. As far as lifespan is concerned, they live longer than all other monkeys: gibbons can reach the age of fifty while the great apes can even reach the ripe old age of fifty-five.

The gorilla is by far the largest of all the primates, much larger than human beings. A male silverback can weigh as much as 450 pounds (200 kilograms). The females on the other hand weigh only half that. In contrast gibbons are very

> **Gorillas are by nature incredibly peaceful. They are stoical, reserved and introvert. Their entire emotional life is reflected in their soft, dark-brown eyes.**
>
> GEORGE SCHALLER

A RARITY: Fruit is much more rarely on the menu of western gorillas than leaves and green stuff.

lightweight. The smallest ones can weigh as little as 11 to 13 pounds (5 to 6 kilograms), much less their cousins cousins with tails, some of which can even weigh more than 65 pounds (30 kilograms).

Almost everything is possible in the social life of the great apes. Orangutans, especially adult males, go through life mostly on their own. Gibbons, on the other hand, live mostly in a one-to-one monogamous relationship. Couples, once they have formed, remain together for life. The usual social structure of the gorilla is the harem: a big, powerful, impressive silverback usually has over twenty females but he often also tolerates

younger males in the group. The social structure of chimpanzees is different again. They live in large groups of usually over fifty individuals (in extreme cases as many as three times that). The structure of the group is subject to a strict hierarchy. The members do not always remain together; they come and go, seeing other members perhaps every few days or weeks.

As far as diet is concerned, all great apes are very fond of fruit. They usually know exactly where particular fruit become ripe in their region. Orangutans can open large fruit with hard shells while chimpanzees use tools that they make

COMMITMENT: You can always rely on mother—and this is particularly true of orangutans, here the lighter-colored species of Sumatra.

themselves. They also ferret termites out of their nests and often hunt monkeys, excitedly dividing the raw flesh amongst themselves. In contrast gorillas have a rather meager diet. They eat wild celery stems, nettle leaves and other green stuff, but they eat a lot of it each day. While chimpanzees have been divided into two species for a long time, the divisions of gorillas and orangutans into two species each is relatively recent.

With the new classification the number of our closest relatives has become more extensive.

In the case of gibbons, a classification more strictly based on genetics has led to the identification of further species; instead of two genera, there are now four and the number of species has been increased from seven to nineteen. The number of our closest relatives has become more extensive. But all of them are endangered to a greater or lesser extent. Fortunately the trade in young animals has substantially decreased. Because the mothers and often others were killed in acquiring the young, nine great apes died for each one that ended up alive in captivity.

This is why a long time ago zoos completely stopped importing animals captured in the wild. Nevertheless small gorillas or orangutans are still seized by the authorities, while the stages of reintroducing young animals are still in progress. The trade in "bush meat" (chimpanzees and gorilla for the pot) has not stopped. But much more disastrous is the fact that man is changing the great apes' habitat, making it harder for them to

A CHARACTER FULL OF CONTRASTS: The bonobos are the most spirited of our close relatives but they can also be pensive.

exist. Palm oil plantations are constantly spreading where in the past gibbons and orangutans used to have their rain forests. Thanks to Jane Goodall and many others, today we understand our closest relatives much better. We have even accepted them zoologically in our family. But living with us has made their lives much harder.

If we don't do something very soon,
our closest relatives will only
survive in captivity. JANE GOODALL

WHITE BROWS
Hoolock hoolock

....

▪ Northeast India, Bangladesh

....

A young male western hoolock gibbon (in females the entire face is surrounded by white) in a flowering mango tree. It will still have to wait a while before it can enjoy the fruits (bottom left).

GREY BROWN
Hylobates funereus

....

▪ North and East Borneo

....

Because they mostly swing along branches, gibbons rarely have their hands free. That is why this Eastern Borneo gibbon is not carrying its baby in its arm but on its thigh (bottom right).

JET-BLACK
Symphalangus syndactylus

....

▪ Malaysia, Sumatra

....

In the siamang family, the largest of the gibbons, both males and females are black. Using its throat pouch—which only they have— they can sing very loudly, but not necessarily beautifully (right).

LONG-ARMED
Hylobates albibarbis

▪ Southwest Borneo

*Of all the primates the gibbons
have the longest arms. This is
evident in the white-bearded
gibbon which, weighing only
15 pounds (7 kilograms) at the
most, does not need much
strength for swinging in the
trees. To do this it only needs
to be wiry and sinewy.*

Man is more a monkey than many a monkey.

FRIEDRICH NIETZSCHE

A PLAY OF COLOR
Nomascus annamensis

▪ South Laos, Northeast Cambodia, Vietnam

The male and female northern yellow-cheeked gibbon have different coloring. The males are black while the females are beige to near-white with a black marking on the head. At birth they are pale, then both sexes grow black fur. It is only when they reach adulthood that the females become pale-colored again (top left).

WELL-TRIMMED
Hylobates albibarbis

▪ Southwest Borneo

Even a hairdresser could not trim the beard of this white-bearded gibbon any better. Whiskers are always best looked after without comb and scissors. (bottom left).

BLACK CAP
Hylobates pileatus

▪ Southeast Thailand, Laos, Cambodia

Both male and female piliated gibbons have a white ring of hair round the black cap. But while the female is grey, the male is black. In fact, most male and female gibbons differ in color (bottom right).

WHITE HANDS
Hylobates lar

▪ Laos, Thailand, Malaysia, North Sumatra

The white-handed gibbons or lars do not go for color differences. In their case both males and females may be either black or beige. The couples know each other and stay together for the long haul, irrespective of the color of their partner (right).

Social life

Among primates anything is possible

Lifelong faithfulness hardly exists in the animal kingdom. There are exceptions such as geese and cranes—and among the primates, gibbons. When a couple has formed, they remain together for life. In their case this can mean decades. They indicate their living quarters to the outside world by singing together. As a result every member of the species knows that this is where a harmonious couple lives and that they should stay away from there. When children are born, they seek their own partner.

Orangutans think little of such communal life. Males and females have their own territorie which may overlap. If a female is ready to conceive, the male will stay with her for a few days. Then he wanders off alone. Only mothers and their children form strong communities. Similarly anti-social prosimians are galagos, loris and nocturnal Madagascar lemurs.

Most primates are incredibly gregarious and sociable and live mainly in family groups of about a dozen members. Baboons, rhesus monkeys and capuchin monkeys live in larger groups which may number between twenty and fifty members. But those who form the largest groups are the gelada baboons which frequently live in groups of up to a hundred animals. All these groups are based on a strict hierarchy—both among males and females. Daughters often inherit their mother's status but sons must fight their way up—in the literal sense of the word. In most pri-

UNUSUAL: Like all their relatives, the white-bearded gibbons form lifelong couples.

mate-communities it is the males who call the shots. But there are exceptions: in the case of the Madagascar ring-tailed lemur the females are definitely the stronger sex.

Several species of primates such as langurs, proboscis monkeys, hamadryas baboons and gorillas have developed a harem structure as a way of life. A powerful male will surround itself with a group of females. Usually this male is the only one to procreate. In the case of gorillas a silverback male can lead a harem for decades. In contrast, the Indian langurs must constantly fight to keep their females. Gangs of young males are forever challenging the "boss" in an attempt to depose it in battles that are often bloody. If they succeed, the new leaders will first kill all the very young babies so that the mothers will be ready to conceive again more quickly.

LOVING GROOMING: Especially among chimpanzees who live a fairly loose family life, grooming is very important to ensure cohesion in the group.

FEMININE
Nomascus leucogenys

▪ South China, North Vietnam, Northwest Laos

A female northern white-cheeked gibbon: light-colored fur and a black top of head, looking a little fierce. But that is only directed at the photographer. The look to its lifelong partner as a couple would be much more friendly.

MASCULINE
Nomascus leucogenys

▪ South China, North Vietnam, Northwest Laos

Northern white-cheeked gibbon, male: black fur, white whiskers— kind and trusting. But the future of this gibbon species looks anything but rosy. Because of persecution and loss of habitat it is considered seriously endangered.

Pongo pygmaeus

▪ Borneo

Of all the great apes the two orangutan species are the most likely to live as loners. But the love and affection for the young is all the greater and deeper: the young stay close their mother for a good five years and learn everything they need from her (left and right).

NESTLING
Pongo pygmaeus

▪ Borneo

The average interval between two births of a Borneo orangutan female is about six to eight years. The elder child is often still with its mother when the next baby is being breastfed. It is only at the age of seven or eight, often together with two or three other youngsters, that they go their own way. The females have their first baby at the age of about fifteen and they usually become pregnant only four or five times in their life (186-187).

INTIMACY
Pongo pygmaeus

▪ Borneo

For five years orangutan mothers do little else but look after their baby. Because there are no tigers on Borneo, these large great apes have no serious enemies—with the exception of human beings. Where they are allowed to keep their habitat, there is plenty of food for these primates and they are not picky at all. As a result they have plenty of time to look after their young on whom they lavish love and affection.

LOUDMOUTH
Pongo pygmaeus

▪ Borneo

Male orangutans are not only twice as large as the females, they also differ in having cheek bulges that serve mainly to impress. In the case of the Borneo orangutan they are relatively heavy and hang towards the front while those of the Sumatra males are flatter and hairier.

HEAVY WEIGHT
Pongo pygmaeus

▪ Borneo

Orangutans are the heaviest animals that live permanently in the trees. As they get older males can reach 220 pounds (100 kilograms). Nevertheless they are extremely agile climbers. The throat pouch, clearly visible in this animal, serves as sound amplifier when the males sing to mark their territory, and this only occurs rarely.

Aggression

Life: a permanent struggle

Once Jane Goodall had come to know her chimpanzees extremely well, she became convinced that they were in fact the better people. Naturally they had arguments and conflicts but these were usually followed by a reconciliation. But then something happened that completely destroyed her idea of chimpanzees. For three years the males in her research group attacked their rivals in the neighborhood at regular intervals. The strange thing about this was that these were old acquaintances which had left the group and formed their own unit. The attacks were so fierce that the victims were seriously injured and could not be found again, in spite of the scientists' searching. In the end the new group was completely destroyed. Certainly, such a "war" among non-human primates is an extremely rare occurrence. Observing it was only possible because the Gombe chimpanzees were followed at every turn by Jane Goodall and many other scientists. But the fact is that monkeys are generally quite aggressive with each other. This picture is not improved by the fact gorillas are generally described as gentle giants—because they are extraordinarily peaceful amongst themselves but also towards people (unlike the "King Kong" image presented in the movie).

On the whole there are no strict rules among primates when it comes to conflicts. With many hoofed

AN INTIMIDATING SIGHT: When a male gelada baboon bares its teeth and curls its lips, enemies are terrified.

animals innate behavior patterns ensure that they do not hurt themselves seriously, but monkeys do not know about such ritualized fighting. They not only bite unrestrainedly: they also hit out with their hands and feet. But this happens very rarely. After all, members of a group know each other very well. Everyone knows their rank and that it is best not to interfere with the established order. And there are well-known signals of appeasement in order not to challenge the stronger ones. Rival groups are warned off loudly with sounds that declare that this territory is occupied, others have no business here. So the intruders go away and a fight is avoided. But when it comes down to it, monkeys are anything but restrained.

SHOWING-OFF: the chest thumping of a male gorilla is the most famous threatening gesture in the animal kingdom.

**The more you learn about
the dignity of the gorilla,
the more you want
to avoid people.**

DIAN FOSSEY

IMPOSING
Gorilla beringei

▪ East Congo, Southwest Uganda,
Northwest Ruanda

*To stand only 30 feet (10 meters)
in front of such a mountain gorilla
as this is absolutely breathtaking.
Yet it is not dangerous because
it is rightly known to be a gentle
giant (right).*

FRUGAL
Gorilla beringei

▪ East Congo, Southwest Uganda,
Northwest Ruanda

*The meager diet the largest
primates have to manage on is
quite remarkable: the male Eastern
or Mountain gorillas can weigh
over 440 pounds (200 kilograms)
and yet it feeds almost exclusively
on leaves (here nettle leaves), bark
and stems (bottom left).*

DOMINANT
Gorilla beringei

▪ East Congo, Southwest Uganda,
Northwest Ruanda

*It is clear who is the boss in this
family: the male silverback is not
only twice as tall an twice as heavy
as its wives but it also decides what
is to happen throughout the day,
for instance, when it is time to rest
and when it is time to move on
(198-199).*

Dangers

How are the primates threatened?

Fortunately monkeys do not have the kind of fur that ladies would like to wear, no horns or bones used for medicinal purposes, nor ivory for piano keys. As a result monkeys are not hunted and exterminated like tigers, elephants and rhinos. The days when they were used as jesters at court or kept in cages as cute animals are long past. Also guereza fur jackets have gone completely out of fashion. Until the early 20th century this fashion cost the lives of millions of guereza monkeys.

Also the trade in such wild animals has disappeared. In the past, for each orangutan or gorilla that landed in a zoo, nine lost their lives in the process, because the mother would be shot and most of the young did not survive the brutal capture and inadequate care. Today zoos are so good at breeding animals that they are able to send some of them back to their natural habitat. The reintroduction program is also proving successful with golden lion-tailed monkeys.

Nevertheless there are still dangers threatening our relatives. The problem is not Indians or pygmies hunting the primates for meat. The real problem is that the forest, home to 90 percent of the species, is constantly shrinking. The forest is cleared to provide space for cattle grazing (supplying the meat in our hamburgers), or for palm oil plantations. There is no room for the monkeys any more. Gorillas and chim-

FASHION MONKEY: While they used to be hunted for their fur, today guereza monkeys are threatened by their shrinking habitat.

panzees have long been hunted and eaten. Today they are still on the menu as "bush meat" in the restaurants of the expanding towns.

Most of the 100 lemur species in Madagascar are under threat although broadly speaking they are no longer hunted. But their already small habitat is shrinking by the day. At the same time, new species continue to be discovered and described, albeit a very small number in isolated, tiny areas. The new species are listed as endangered at the same moment as they are first described.

Most primates are losing their habitat. It is being stolen from them by their dominant relative, man.

DARING: Like its relatives, the western gorilla cannot swim. But that does not stop it getting into the water.

The
alrea
base
were
excit
we tr
and I
get to
had to
was m
double

From "Ape Lady" to Dame Jane

The behavior of our closest relatives has been studied for over 100 years, from the mouse lemurs to the gorillas. Publications on the subject would fill entire libraries. Among the "classics" are the studies by Japanese primatologists who described the "monkey culture" of red-faced macaques for the first time, and George Schaller's famous study on mountain gorillas, to mention just two of the most important.

Research on our closest relatives, the chimpanzees, also dates back many years. One of the pioneers was Wolfgang Köhler. Between 1913 and 1917 he carried out specific studies with chimpanzees and for the first time reported their use of tools. The Americans Robert Yerkes and his wife Ada carried out long-term studies between 1929 and 1942 on up to 90 chimpanzees in their own research laboratory. Also famous are the comparative studies between chimpanzees and human babies carried out by the Russian scientist Nadie Kohts and the American Kellogg husband and wife team. The studies of Dutchman Adriaan Kortlandt who observed chimpanzees from a hideout and showed them stuffed leopards as part of his research were widely popular and publicized in the media. Also worth mentioning are the long-term studies by Christoph Boesch and his students in the Tai National Park in the Ivory Coast.

But all this has been eclipsed by the lifetime achievement over fifty years of the British anthropologist Jane Goodall. In 1960 the anthropologist Louis Leakey sent his young secretary to Gombe on the eastern shore of Lake Tanganyika (now Tanzania) to study chimpanzees. He did the same thing with two other "ape ladies," Dian Fossey for the mountain gorillas and Birute Galdikas for the orangutans.

It took a long time before Jane was accepted by "her" chimpanzees. But once she had been, her new observations caused a sensation. They completely changed the received image people had of anthropoid monkeys: the use of tools (getting termites out with a stick), the organized hunting for colobus and much more. With the results of her research she was wrote a doctoral thesis which earned her a Ph.D degree from Cambridge University.

The "Jane Goodall Institute" which she founded in 1977 was funded with the money of her work. Many students who were guided by her with great patience helped with practical things, as they still do today. After about a quarter of a century Jane Goodall decided to devote herself entirely to public relations activities on behalf of chimpanzees and the preservation of nature. To do this she travels around the world for almost 300 days reach year. Her youth organization "Roots and Shoots" now has offshoots in many countries throughout the world.

Among the numerous awards Jane Goodall has received, two stand out. She has been appointed a DBE, Dame Commander of the British Empire, and also a UN peace ambassadress by Kofi Annan: well-deserved recognition of a remarkable life's work.

WORLD RECORD: The chimpanzees in the Gombe Stream National Park in Tanzania have been studied for over fifty years.

Galagoides rondoensis | *Rondo dwarf galago*
Galagoides granti | *Mozambique dwarf galago*
Galagoides cocos | *Kenya coast dwarf galago*
Galagoides zanzibaricus | *Tanzania coast dwarf galago*

GREATER GALAGO – OTOLEMUR

With a snout-to-vent length of almost 20 inches (50 centimeters) and a weight of up to 4 1/2 pounds (2 kilograms), the greater galagos of eastern and southern Africa is considerably larger than the usual bushbabies. Unlike the latter, they rarely leap but instead move by scrambling on four legs. Stronger than their smaller relatives, they feed on fruit and do not live as loners but in small family groups of up to six.

→ *2 species*
Otolemur crassicaudatus | *Thick-tailed greater galago*
Otolemur garnettii | *Garnett's greater galago*

BIOKO ALLEN'S BUSHBABY – SCIUROCHEIRUS

Bioko Allen's bushbabies are more closely-related to the greater galagos than to the actual galagos and are therefore a species in their own right. They feed mainly on fruit and tree sap, less on insects and vertebrae. What they all have in common are gigantic eyes and ears. They live mainly in the Central African rain forest.

→ *3 species*
Sciurocheirus alleni | *Bioko squirrel galago*
Sciurocheirus cameronensis | *Cross River squirrel galago*
Sciurocheirus gabonensis | *Gabon squirrel galago*

NEEDLE-CLAWED BUSHBABY – EUOTICUS

The needle-clawed bushbabies are highly adapted to feeding on tree saps. They have claw-like nails and large incisors pointing forward that enable them to gnaw at the tree bark. Like the other galagos they are territorial and mark their territory with their urine. They often spend the night in small groups but always go food-hunting on their own. They only occur in a small area in central Africa.

→ *2 species*
Euoticus pallidus | *Northern needle-clawed bushbaby*
Euoticus elegantulus | *Southern needle-clawed bushbaby*

Lorisidae family (lorises)

ANGWANTIBOS – ARCTOCEBUS

The tailless angwantibos, 9 to 12 inches (22 to 30 centimeters) long, only occur in the Central African rainforest of Nigeria and Cameroun as far as Gabon. At night they clamber slowly through the lower branches of trees in search of insects, especially caterpillars. They only rarely improve their diet with fruit. The mother carries her new-born young on her front but she often hangs them on a branch when she goes looking for food.

→ *2 species*
Arctocebus calabariensis | *Calabar angwantibo*
Arctocebus aureus | *Golden angwantibo*

POTTO – PERODICTICUS

The potto weighs up to 3 pounds (1.3 kilograms) and so belongs to the larger representatives of the African and Asian loris prosimians. The snout-to-vent length is 12 to 16 inches (30 to 40 centimeters) and the stumpy tail is at most 4 inches (10 centimeters) long. They live in the tropical African rainforest from Guinea to western Kenya. During their cautious night-time forays pottos feed mainly on fruit and less on tree sap and insects. They are territorial and quarrelsome with congeners of the same sex.

→ *3 species*
Perodicticus potto | *West African potto*
Perodicticus edwardsi | *Milne-Edwards's potto*
Perodicticus ibeanus | *East African potto*

GREY SLENDER LORIS – LORIS

Grey slender lorises are relatively small, graceful primates, at most 9 inches (22 centimeters) long. These tailless prosimians live in eastern and southern India andSri Lanka. At night they scramble slowly through the undergrowth of their forests. Their diet consists mainly of insects but they will also eat small vertebrae and plants.

→ *2 species*
Loris lydekkerianus | *Gray slender loris*
Loris tardigradus | *Red slender loris*

SLOW LORIS – NYCTICEBUS

Slow lorises, widespread in large parts of south-east Asia (from India and China to Borneo and Java) are clearly sturdier and

HAPPY: Borneo orangutans.

Behind the camera

Thomas Marent: Rain forest challenge

I t was when I visited a rain forest for the first time in Eastern Australia in 1990 that it happened to me: the air there is always warm and humid, the vegetation is lush and dense and everywhere things are creaking and rustling. This unique universe has never relinquished its hold on me. It harbors about 70 percent of all animal and plant species that exist on land. So no wonder that for a nature photographer like me these regions around the equator are among the most exciting on earth.

For 25 years now I have been traveling around rain forests and photographed their fauna in Asia, Latin America, Africa, Australia and New Zealand. At the same time I naturally recorded the threat to our "green lungs." Every year large parts of this priceless eco-system disappear. Between 2000 and 2010 an area the size of Switzerland disappeared every year. Most of our closest relatives live in the large rain forests and quite large numbers of species are seriously endangered because of their shrinking habitat. Over the last few years I have concentrated my photographic work on primates. By showing the great diversity of our closest relatives, I wanted to highlight the importance of diversity for the genera and species.

Work in the rain forest is exciting but it is also a real challenge. Apart from the high humidity, the weight of the equipment and the troublesome mosquitoes and ants, it is often very difficult to find a good subject. The animals are shy—and with good reason: in many regions they are still being hunted. And so it sometimes happened that after a strenuous day in the rain forest, I returned to my quarters without having taken a single picture of a monkey.

Two years ago, when I visited the northern Amazon region in Brazil during the rainy season to photograph the white Uakaria monkeys, the forests were flooded for several months. So I travelled around by canoe for days—in vain. It was only on the last day that I finally found the subject I had been looking for. I took up my position with my heavy 600-mm lens and the 1.7x converter in the narrow rocking canoe—and at the back of my mind was the constant fear of falling into the water with my equipment. Then I pressed the button with my shaking hand. A successful picture (page 86) was the reward for my patience. These moments have made up for all the trouble and effort.

In order to take these photograph, I had to overcome a lot of obstacles and hurdles—and I

Top left *Picture-stalking in the Tanjung Puting National Park in Indonesia, home to about 6,000 orangutans.*
Top center *The red-backed saki in Guyana is extremely shy. Fortunately it was tempted by the ripe fruit in front of my lens.*
Top right *The fascinating golden snub-nosed monkeys in the Qinling Mountains, Shaanxi, China.*

Bottom left *A threatening gesture—better not to get too close the geladas for the moment.*
Bottom center *In search of the rare black Delacour's langur in the Van Long Nature Reserve, Vietnam.*
Bottom right *Vervet Monkey, baby, in the Masai Mara National Reserve, Kenya.*

would not have succeeded without the support of many people who made things easier for me in one way or other. In particular I want to thank my parents, Rose and Richard Marent (Switzerland). I would also like to thank the following people and organizations: David Weiller (France), Tom Swensson (Sweden), Jeremy Holden (England), André Stapfer (Switzerland), Urs Jaschke (Switzerland), Sylvia Dudek (Canada), Andrew and Margaret Ingles (Australia), Karina Najera (Mexico), Carlos Andrés Galvis (Colombia), Noemí Kubota (Brazil), Biswajit Guha (Singapore), Abhishek Jain (India), Yvonne A. de Jong (Kenya), Ulrike Streicher of "Fauna & Flora International" (www.fauna-flora.org) in Vietnam, Erik Patel of "Duke Lemur Center SAVA Conservation" in Madagascar (www.lemur.duke.edu/conservation), Liza Gadsby of "Pandrillus Foundation" in Nigeria (www.pandrillus.org), Qi Xiao-Guang "College of Life Science" in China, Baoping Ren of the Zoological Institute of the "Chinese Academy of Sciences" in Peking, Gudrun Sperrer "Amazon Animal Orphanage" in Peru (www. amazonanimalorphanage.org), of the "Rainforest Foundation Norway" and"Lola Ya Bonobo" in the Congo (www.friendsofbonobos.org) and "Piedad Mejia" in Colombia.

Thomas Marent

The Swiss photographer **Thomas Marent**, born in Baden in 1966, has been traveling in the tracks of the most fascinating animals in the world for over thirty years. Since he first visited the rain forest in Australia in 1990, this immensely species-rich habitat has been his particular interest, a fascination that has drawn him to the rain forests of Asia, Latin America, Africa, Australia and New Zealand. While traveling in the most remote areas of our planet, Thomas Marent has documented the biodiversity of primates.

He photographs our closest relatives in their natural habitats, but these are increasingly disappearing and threatening the survival of several species. In addition to his work as a nature photographer Thomas Marent also carries out monitoring of butterflies, dragonflies and grasshoppers, and since 2013 he has led nature photo tour workshops in various areas of rain forest. Find out more at www.thomasmarent.com

Fritz Jantschke, is a zoologist and a journalist. After completing his PhD on the behavior of orangutans he was curator at the Frankfurt Zoo, focusing on public relations. Then he worked as editor of the animal magazine *Das Tier* and recently he has produced many wildlife films for television. Subjects have included primates, from orangutans and proboscis monkeys in Borneo to lemurs in Madagascar, chimpanzees in Uganda, drills in Nigeria and lion tamarins in Brazil. Find out more at www.fritz-jantschke.de

Managing editor: Dorothea Sipilä
Editing, layout and typesetting: VerlagsService Dr. Helmut Neuberger & Karl Schaumann GmbH, Kirchheim
Cover design and layout concept: coverdesign uhlig,
Augsburg
Repro: Ludwig, Zell am See

© 2014 Frederking & Thaler Verlag in der Bruckmann Verlag GmbH, Munich

WHITE STAR PUBLISHERS

WS White Star Publishers® is a registered trademark
property of De Agostini Libri S.p.A.

© 2014 De Agostini Libri S.p.A.
Via G. da Verrazano, 15
28100 Novara, Italy
www.whitestar.it - www.deagostini.it

Translation and Editing: Rosetta Translations SARL

ISBN 978-88-544-0890-6
1 2 3 4 5 6   18 17 16 15 14

Printed in China

All the facts in this book have been carefully researched and updated as well as being proofread by the publisher. However, no liability can be assumed for the accuracy of the content.

All photographs © Thomas Marent, except the following pictures:
page 7 © picture-alliance/Bernd Kammerer, page 17 © picture-alliance/Everett Collection,
page 19 © picture-alliance/WILDLIFE, page 239 (top left) © Nathalie Senn,
page 239 (top right) © David Weiller, page 239 (top center) © Jeremy Holden.

Cover: Impressive male golden snub-nosed monkey.
Back cover from top right to bottom left: Liszt monkey, Japan macaque, Drill monkey, Black snub-nosed monkey.
Photographs by: © Thomas Marent